HEALING Tl
SELF

FREEDOM FROM STATES OF MIND AND
MENTAL ILLNESS

J. F. GORDON

PHILADELPHIA BOOKS
"See, I have set before you an open door that no-one can shut"

1

ISBN 978-0-9570970-6-3

"The time is fulfilled," Jesus said, "and the kingdom of God is at hand. Repent and believe the good news!"

Mark 1:15, composite quotation.

"Rescue those being led astray to death; hold back those staggering towards slaughter. If you say, "But we knew nothing about this," does not he who weighs the heart perceive it? Does not he who guards your life know it? Will he not repay each person according to what he has done?"

Proverbs 24:11-12.

CONTENTS

FOREWORD

I was both honoured and delighted to be asked to write a Foreword to Dr. Gordon's book *Healing the Divided Self.* For it is both a very unusual and a very good book.

It is unusual to find a book written by an experienced psychiatrist which sources from Scripture the foundational principles which undergird the thinking; and it is a very good book because what Dr. Gordon has written is an outstanding treatise taking both theologian and medical professional on a rich journey of understanding for which I, personally, am very grateful.

Both medics and theologians will be challenged by the truths and arguments presented in these pages. The ancient creedal beliefs of the Church form the spiritual foundation for the teaching and while medics may be reluctant to accept that such spiritual matters can be relevant to a modern-day healing model, I urge those who really care for their patients as 'people' as opposed to 'clients', to lay aside any sense of scepticism and ask themselves honest questions about the relevance of what they are reading to the people they are seeking to help. When they look at the answers this book provides they may well be very surprised to discover that their belief in God and what He has said through His Word is more believable, relevant and important than they could have ever imagined!

I also urge those theologians and Christian Pastors who have hesitated to take up their responsibility to care for the healing needs of their sheep (see Ezekiel 34), in favour of automatically referring their people in need for professional psychiatric help, to think again. This psychiatrist wisely says that *"there is always more to our condition than medicine can resolve."*

One of the most profound statements that Dr. Gordon makes is *"being with others as they find their healing can challenge you to find yours."* How utterly true this is. The fact is we are all in need of healing and it can be a very humbling experience to look at ourselves in the mirror provided by those who God asks us to help. Unless we rise to the task of helping others we may never truly discover our real self.

Just as the work of healing cannot be separated from the work of making disciples – if you try and practice psychiatric medicine without any understanding of the spiritual nature of man, the consequences of sin and the inner damage that can be caused by others, your medical model will, by definition, be seriously deficient. And if you try and make disciples without any understanding of their healing needs you will discover that your work is always undermined by the unhealed inner realities of people who may want to be disciples, but are constantly held back by their own limitations and, as a result, will never rise to the fulfilment of their true identity in Christ.

I would urge both medics and Christian leaders to take time out to study seriously *Healing the Divided Self*. It is one of the most profound books I have read in many a year and I will be strongly recommending it as important reading for all those we work with in the ministry of Christian healing.

Peter Horrobin, M.A.(Oxon.). March 2015.
Founder and International Director
Ellel Ministries International.

PREFACE

Generally it seems taken for granted that human experience and behaviour that is distressing or reckoned mad is best investigated and treated through the scientific disciplines of psychology and psychiatry.[1] But the work of some philosophers tacitly questions the adequacy of this assumption.[2]

Christian theologians, however, have failed to take the philosophical bait. In consequence, theology has failed to interpret Scripture in a sufficiently real and substantial way so as to extend Christian faith into the uncomfortable field of healing for emotional and mental suffering, pain and confusion. It has been easier to institute rules for Christian living and to diagnose indigence, mental illness or criminality in those who appear incorrigible. Effectively categorized, intransigent people are then consigned to secular management and treated with condescension, which often masquerades as help.

So whenever experience or behaviour seem abnormal, according to the academic, humanistic sciences to which we commonly look for the elimination of every apparent defect, a person becomes classified, diagnosed, psychologized and medicalized. Secular authorities have evolved administrative systems for dealing with disturbances of the soul by classifying

---

[1] See any standard medical textbook.
[2] Such as Hegel (1807) *The Phenomenology of Mind*; Kierkegaard (1849) *The Sickness unto Death*; James (1902) *Varieties of Religious Experience*; Husserl (1913) *Ideas: General Introduction to Pure Phenomenology*; Sartre (1956) *Being and Nothingness*; Heidegger (1959) *Being and Time*; Laing (1967) *The Politics of Experience*; Foucault (1961, full English translation 2006) *History of Madness*.

them as illnesses and disorders of personality in need of treatment. Places and means for their management are allocated and trusted. This is done for the sake of keeping civic peace and public order in a secular world. Although the practice of various faiths is usually permitted, secularists fail to recognize the power of spiritual influence to effect personal change and healing and the development of maturity.

Yet if a person should refuse to be invalidated, and instead call to Messiah Jesus for healing, take their personal experience to him, hear God's word with true discernment, embark upon a process of "demolishing arguments and every pretension that sets itself up against the knowledge of God, and taking captive every thought to make it obedient to Christ" (2 Corinthians 10:5), then secular science and technology may be subordinated to the activity of the Holy Spirit. Drugs and treatments of this world may then cease to be necessary for some people whose true experience is addressed in the light of God's word in the sort of community where neighbours are loved as one's self.

There are radical social implications, particularly with regard to the nature and order of church fellowship.

Meeting the issues raised by alleged madness challenges respectability. We may find that we ourselves, individually, have a lot of inner personal uncertainties for the Lord to heal before we can be hospitable to other people who disturb us. Although we may have devoted our lives to Jesus, we may still be wounded sinners oppressed by wrong relationships and demons. And if this should be the case, those deemed mentally ill should no longer be considered exceptions.

For those who will seriously take hold of the Lord Jesus Christ and enter into a personal relationship with him there is a way that is not of this world.

There has been too much secular worldliness in the church for too long, and too much unbelief. Out of the realisation that sickness and disease are connected with issues that can be put right with God through accepting Jesus, comes richer understanding of the word of God that enables it to become vitally incorporated into everyday language. The healing activity of the Holy Spirit can set a person free of prejudices and strongholds of the mind so as to be able to meet other people with love in sincerity and truth. And if followers of Jesus are going to be salt and light in this world they need the empathy to know what is in other people, as Jesus did (John 2:25), and to address them in language full of grace, seasoned with salt (Colossians 4:6).

The Father wants his churches to curtail their emphasis on entertainment and to stop assuming that people change by being programmed like computers. He desires to heal his people through personal relationship, to rid us of everything that gets in the way of knowing him personally, hearing his voice in our hearts and taking him seriously in every aspect of our lives, so that collectively we may reflect his presence. He desires his churches to be places of sincere fellowship, refuges from the storm of virtual reality and secular meaninglessness for those he is bringing into his kingdom and transforming into a holy priesthood to join him always for ever.

Therefore this book assumes belief in the great creeds of the Christian church, in the reality of Jesus' resurrection, in the new birth (John 3:3) and in the supernatural, sanctifying activity of Holy Spirit. It assumes acceptance that "All Scripture is given by inspiration of God" (2 Timothy 3:16, KJV) and that living faith in the Lord Jesus Christ of Nazareth includes repentance, forgiveness of confessed sin, personal acceptance of redemption through the shed blood of Jesus and his victory on the cross, and of his incomparably great power for us who believe.

Together with my book *'Healing for the Wounded Life,'* this is a contribution towards making up a deficiency in the current theological understanding of the nature of mankind. The extent of the deficiency may become more apparent as secular health and welfare services become stretched to the limit and too expensive to support.

11

1

SOCIAL REALITIES

Going crazy?

If ever you are seriously worried about being excessively stressed, confused, or emotionally overburdened, or if your inability to control your behaviour seems to be distressing other people too much, you may perhaps take yourself along to the doctor.

Quite commonly, though, the people you live or work with will be suspecting that you may be becoming mentally ill, and they may therefore suggest that you should seek professional help. They may even go out of their way to make sure you get it, whether you want it or not.

The actual account you seem to give them when you tell them what you think and feel, and what you are doing, may not reassure them sufficiently. People may therefore feel naturally anxious about you. And if, after getting to know you a little better, they then begin to feel even more worried and unsafe about you, they may assume that there is definitely something wrong with you. And that can be the beginning of having things done to you that you may not want.

You may disagree with their assumptions, but you may nevertheless feel obliged to do as they say, so as not to be rejected by them. A medical diagnosis may satisfy them. If so, it is important to remember that you need not give up hope of making yourself fully understood by them in plain, non-technical language. If the doctor says you are mentally ill, however, other people will tend to believe it. The stigma and label can sometimes prove hard to shake off.

Taking responsibility

Taking responsibility for yourself involves not only being aware of the effect you have on other people but also being willing to take into account that other people may not understand you properly.

The most common reason why people do not understand this sort of thing is that your distress reverberates inside them and threatens to make them feel distressed, too. And they cannot empathise with you because they are frightened about how to handle that and do not know what to do. Their anxiety may prevent them from fully appreciating your meaning. So they may feel uncomfortably constrained to find words for concepts they have never been able really to consider. You may even be causing them to have to begin to remember painful personal events that they put out of mind unhealed long ago.

People will not usually acknowledge this sort of thing, and they will prefer instead to put on a respectable face and not admit to being unable to understand you, or to not knowing how to respond to you. Consequently you may easily feel rejected because no one seems able to comprehend the truth of what you are saying. No one will meet you. But do not expect anyone to acknowledge that they are actually rejecting you. On the contrary, they will think they are doing the very best thing. After all, without Jesus they are probably unable to do anything other than judge. So from then on they will effectively dictate the terms for mutual understanding if they can. And they will effectively exclude subjects that may urgently matter to you.

If you do not forgive such people right from the start, you can become too hurt, too frightened, or too embittered, to take the trouble to bother to account for yourself truthfully any longer. It may seem counter-productive to disturb their peace too much because, in consequence, they could hurt you more. Desperate to be taken seriously by somebody but, in fact, met by nobody, you can easily become despondent.

How to find courage

It is best to use language that does not cause too much offence, and to accept the risk that you will probably not be fully understood. After all, God knows what you are suffering (Hebrews 4:13). No matter how offended you yourself may be, the best way to avoid having unwanted things done to you, is to listen to God, renounce your pride, be forgiving and stop expecting genuine help, or justice, from people who do not understand, no matter how nice or important they may seem. It is quite surprising to discover who fails to understand. But it is also surprising to discover how God is able and willing to help and heal you (Psalm 109:31).

Although you may long to have someone to talk to, and to be sincerely and truthfully met by another human being who understands, no human being with sufficient maturity may be available. Even those by whom you might expect to be helped, such as church leaders or doctors, may fail to connect with you. You may just find the gumption, however, to speak to God in the name of Messiah Jesus, and to allow God himself to speak to you quietly through his Holy Spirit. If you accept God's only begotten Son Jesus for your saviour He will come to live in you. Holy Spirit can open up the truth to you with the help of the word of God in the Bible. The Holy Bible is the very best textbook. Truth revealed by Holy Spirit and the word of God is often painful. It may seem to conflict with what most people believe. There are layers of revelation. But you will not need scientific psychology.

Submit to God and be discerning about people

If you take no account of anyone else and refuse to be accountable for yourself in terms that the people around you are willing and able to accept, however, you will probably have to contend with other people's sanctions against you. It can be very distressing to be unable to make sense about vital personal matters with other people on whom you depend. Not to have an intelligible response from them can easily make you despair. But if the way your distress is expressed is too disturbing for other people they will take measures to make you conform. If you worry them because they do not understand you and believe you lack self-control, they may try to do something to you that you do not want in order to control you.

In turn, you, yourself, may or may not be inclined to understand anyone who finds you distressing. And you may or may not realise how distressing you are to other people, just as they may not realise how distressing they are to you. So perhaps a referee or advocate may be needed for each side, so that each may to begin to hear the other. Policemen, nurses and psychiatrists do not always make good referees because they have an administrative job to do. So, if you want a referee, it is best to choose carefully before policemen, nurses or psychiatrists get involved (Matthew 18:15-17, Luke 12:57-59). If you can speak and be truly heard, and if together with others you can make enough sense of it all, there may be no need for further help. But if there is no understanding, you can quickly feel most distressingly alienated.

Rejection

Being rejected like this is the commonest event to precipitate a person into breakdown. If rejection is felt as accusation, and if you feel the accusation may actually be justified, you may then begin to condemn yourself for being as you are. But when this is the case there must be something going on in the milieu in which you are living or working that cannot be adequately opened up and brought into the light, something in you, something in them, some real but hidden meaning or influence somewhere. And for you to become, as a result, the one who is apparently ill indicates that you may be vulnerable to this influence. You could be vulnerable because of a similar pattern of events in the past that were never resolved, that remain unhealed somewhere at the back of your mind. In all seriousness, this is worth considering.

There is both a social aspect and also a personal history to every sort of breakdown. It is never totally mad.

Although other people may believe you are the one that needs help, the truth could be that it is what is going on, between yourself and other people and God, which needs to change. In practice, however, it is either the one who has lost self-control, or the one whose demeanour distresses the people who are more powerful, that gets treated as the sick one.

Invalidation

If you are actually diagnosed as ill, your account of what you are experiencing can all too easily become invalidated. Then confusion, frustration and despondency may easily damage your will. If you are not careful, you can gradually cease to have a mind of your own. Therefore it is wise to keep asking yourself, "Who knows the truth? Whose wisdom can really be trusted? Whose wisdom do they trust? How may sound sense be found? Who says what is just? What is true? What is wise? Whose authority will ultimately stand firm?" And ask God in the name of Jesus for the answers. Please read Psalm 94:20 and 1 Corinthians 2:14-16.

A place of safety

If you have not managed to find a safe place, and have not been smart enough to avoid psychiatrists or officers of the law, you may be taken to 'a place of safety' – deemed safe for yourself and others – such as a hospital, or even police custody or a prison. And you may also lose your job, and much more besides. Arrangements will be made for "clinical assessment", and then for some sort of "management" and "treatment," in the hope that you may get "better." Depending on your "symptoms," and "diagnosis," an academically approved management protocol will be put in place so that people can legitimately "treat" you.

It is a hard fact of life that restraint is sometimes necessary if a person's behaviour becomes so extravagant that it seems likely

17

that something worse may happen. People only go dangerously crazy, however, when their spirits cannot be contained within the existing culture and when they lose meaningful accountability with other people. When relationships are distorted and there is too much in the dark that cannot be spoken about, and brought into the light, there is terrible pain, which sometimes cannot be told any other way.

Treatment

Then you may be persuaded to take medication, to go here or there, to take part in this or that programme of treatment. Whether or not you, personally, really want help for yourself, from the doctor or from anyone else, will seem to be of little relevance to others.

Just occasionally, of course, the doctor, the psychologist, the nurse, or some other professional, may by good fortune be the only person with whom it is actually possible to begin to find sense and healing. Some professionals actually manage to find godly enlightenment in spite of their training![3]

Whom do you believe?

You may, of course, truly believe that you are ill and that you need all this. Or you may be trying to believe that you are ill, and that the treatment will be for the best and help to make you well.

It is worth considering that the truth could be that you actually gave up hope a long time ago (perhaps even when you were a child) of ever being known and loved for who you really are, or of finding anyone else with whom to speak openly and truthfully, so as to make sense of how you feel and think. This could even explain to some extent why your behaviour seems strange to other people now.

---

[3] No actual training or teaching can ever be guaranteed to lead to true enlightenment and wisdom. It comes from revelation (John 3:8).

You may have forgotten events that happened to you. There may be gaps in your mind of unthinkable hopelessness and confusion – a deep empty abyss in your soul. Whatever it is, it is possible that your present behaviour could be construed as the only way for you to say something about it and to try to do something about it. And it is worth bearing in mind, furthermore, that a hopeless tendency, which may have been with you since a certain time in the past, may now be making you more tractable, more willing to believe lies. If you have always felt unable to find any way out of your wretchedness you may now inadvertently have become so sorry for yourself that self-pity constantly undermines your endurance. Or you may have become so stressed by trying to cope that you have lost resilience.

If you get angry and frustrated at being managed, or at other people's apparent lack of understanding, this is, at least, a hopeful sign of life. Each one of us needs to muster a certain amount of fight in order to persevere against the pressures of this world. It develops character.

Where does self-control come from?

If you lose self-control, other people will generally not be sympathetic. Then the person likely to become most hurt in the long run is you. Neither excessive bitterness nor excessive misery will induce anyone to take the truth of your experience and your predicament more seriously so as to help you more.

It is much more useful to pray, because God really does know the truth of your predicament, and he will help you if you will come to Jesus, who took your pain on the cross (see Isaiah 53:4-6). God's truth is by no means always what the authorities reckon it to be; but neither (by the same token) is it always what you reckon it to be. To find the soundest sense, you have to be open to God's true revelation. You need ears to hear, and you need the Holy Bible. If you put yourself into God's hands, in the name of Jesus, he will reveal a key and help you to be able to receive it. This way, he begins to set you free (John 8:32) and as you take

19

hold of the words of God and believe them, and apply them to your life, you will discover that he gives you peace and self-control (Galatians 5:23).

Resignation

Of course, if you are compliant with this world's authorities, and accept their diagnosis and treatment without demur, you can gain a label that gives you an excuse for what has happened, with access to medical technology and welfare benefits. This enables you to use the secular system. The drugs available these days often take almost all the symptoms away. "Why suffer?" you may think, "Who says this condition has any meaningful significance? Let me just get rid of the symptoms!" But, whether you like it or not, this will always said and done in a spirit of resignation and cynicism. You can so very easily be tempted to settle for an apparently comfortable life of partial invalidity and dismiss all thought of true healing.

Accountable to whom?

Nowhere in the Holy Bible does it say that God will not hold you accountable for all you do and say because you have a diagnosis of illness. God will not say, "I do not hold you guilty for killing that man because I know you were suffering from schizophrenia". The law of the land may say this but God will not (Leviticus 5:17). God will not overlook your behaviour, or your compliant resignation, just because some doctor labels you ill (Genesis 9:5, Romans 14:7-12, 2 Corinthians 5:10). Nevertheless, be assured that when you fear God, and your confession is truthful and comes from your very heart, God is always most merciful.

Don't give up hope

If, however, God's hand is upon you, it may seem worthwhile to seek God's healing as desperately as you can, despite the seductive benefits of welfare provisions that make you comfortable as you are, and despite the relative absence of people who know about Jesus' healing for this sort of thing. It is best to refuse to give up hope. It is best, even in the face of terrible confusion and opposition, and in spite of drugs that may be given to you, to remain awake enough, with your feet on the ground, to give a truthful account of your thoughts, feelings and behaviour to God, and to wait for his words of direction. His guidance will come as you accept and believe in Jesus, as you read the Bible and offer him worship.

Sometimes you actually have to be desperate and angry enough in order to do serious business with God (e.g. Psalm 13, and Luke 11:5-13; but see Psalm 4:4). And it certainly helps, if at all possible, urgently to seek out someone else to talk to who sufficiently understands. You will actually be able to listen to yourself better, and therefore give a better account to God, if you open up your heart with someone else. Then it becomes easier to find the courage to take responsibility for yourself.

The place of kingdom healing

About one person in a hundred is, or has been, diagnosed as psychotic or schizophrenic. At least one person in ten has had a psychiatric diagnosis at some time in their life. About one person in five in most church congregations takes some sort of regular psychiatric medication like antidepressants, tranquilizers or sleeping pills.

Most of the medical treatment would be unnecessary if it were possible to lay the relevant issues before God, with other Christian people, and wait for his healing. After all, the experiences that cause breakdowns and mental illnesses are all human, although they may sometimes seem hard to understand. The Holy Spirit is the Spirit of Truth and God promises to lead us into all truth (John 16:13). And according to his word, it is reasonable for us to expect the Holy Spirit to lead us in truth into his freedom (2 Corinthians 3:17). The wretchedness that generates mental illness need not be anathema just because it seems impossible to bring it into the light to see what it is. The unspeakable will eventually be spoken by the grace of God. He knows all about it (Hebrews 4:13), and he can heal it surprisingly easily (Hebrews 5:7-9 and 7:24-25, Matthew 11:30).

Care of souls

Which is better: to hold a person safe by filling them with medication, or by incarcerating them some other way; or to hold a person in a generous, faithful, truthful, safe, loving relationship, so that together we may discover what has been going on, bring what has been in the dark into the light, and seek reconciliation with God?[4] Good enough godly relationships can, indeed, sometimes take the place of psychiatric medication. Loving your neighbour as yourself is the most viable alternative to drugs. If what is hidden in the dark can be brought into the light of God's truth, healing can come through our relationships (1John 1:7).

Occasionally, however, some people lose self-control to such an extent that they will test every conventional boundary to see if anything holds, and if anything can hold them. Sometimes bad behaviour may become so exuberant that very tough love is necessary for relationships to be godly, just and truthful. Firm and sometimes forceful handling of other people is on rare occasions absolutely essential for boundaries to remain sound enough to avoid chaos. After all, interpersonal social boundaries are necessary. No one should be violated, and you cannot keep good faith with people if you let them walk all over you.

A new sort of church?

Although Jesus still heals just as he always has done, far too many people fail to gain access to his healing. It is not easy for existing churches to become more hospitable to potentially distressing people who know they want Jesus' help for emotional

---

[4] These themes are discussed in greater detail in my book *Healing for the Wounded Life*, obtainable through Philadelphia Books.

and mental suffering, pain and confusion. How can they adapt their traditions to offer an alternative culture in which the values of this world do not distort truth? New wine may need new wineskins (Matthew 9:17).

So now that the limitations of public health services are becoming ever more obvious, and serious mention of Jesus is all but banned from many of them, how may the followers of Jesus fulfil their duty to heal the sick?

For one thing, space for real repentance is necessary. Repentance can only be adequate when there is safe time and space for it, in God's presence, amongst his people. Paying attention to the sins, wounds, bondages and demons that make the soul and body sick, and to every aspect of real, and sometimes wretched human experience, need not be morbid, because Jesus who lives in us has gained the victory for us over it all. Speaking of painful reality can be grist to the mill for us. We are all sinners. There is real joy in discovering that bringing true facts into the light, and being reconciled to God about them through Jesus, brings healing. If repentance, and our empathy with suffering, should make us grieve, mourn and wail, he will lift us up (James 4:9-10).

For the true church to remain viable, we need house or cell groups that are willing to become accustomed to this sort of thing. They will be called upon to meet some distressing people in these end times, people who are coming to the wedding feast from off the streets. They will need to function as godly healing groups as well as worship, teaching and intercessory groups. It is easily possible for all these functions to run together. If healing should seem too difficult or risky in any particular case, an understanding doctor, nurse, social worker or other professional can usually be found to advise about the extent to which technological medicine may actually be needed. Distress can be contained through facing the truth and keeping faith in loving relationship. Our Lord will always show us how to attend and understand (Luke 8:18) and be hospitable (Romans 12:13) with

23

discernment and wisdom. Painful personal stories need not be excluded from Christian fellowship, no matter how confusing or harrowing. Truth cannot be hidden when there is fear of God. Our desperate dilemmas, difficulties and inner agonies will be used by God to build mature faith amongst his people.

2

THE CENSOR

Living in the living world

We are not taking the fashionable, abstract, sceptical and scientific approach, and remaining in the world of theory. We are instead looking at the sort of thing we people actually perceive and how we naturally respond. With the help of Holy Spirit and the word of God, we have we have been able to make a fair degree of sense of our wide experience of the affairs of human souls. Consequently the headings under which this discussion proceeds will not conform to generally acceptable academic standards. Rather, we are describing ways in which people react in their bodies, souls and spirits, and the effects of our reactions on other people. We are considering the interactions and dynamics of the fallen human world, how we protect ourselves, the mistakes we make, how we become ill and how God may heal us.

We exist in living relation with spiritual powers, people, living creatures, plants, things, and events past and present, and we are responding to them all the time. We are biddable and easily deceived. We become wounded and defend ourselves with pride. And when our responses are not right with God, in whose image we are made (Genesis 1:27), we lack peace.

Consciousness

Sitting at my writing table, I am aware of my hands on my keyboard, and of the words I am writing, and of the keenness of my interest. Having done a lot of homework, I have an assurance of many thoughts at the back of my mind relating to my subject, although I do not become conscious of any of them until they come to mind. I am also aware of the pleasantness of the winter sun that is shining through my window, and I am dimly aware of other events happening in the house. And I know I have just had a conversation with my wife about something else, and I could recall the details if I should need to, and I know I have recently heard the news on the radio but the details of that are no longer in the forefront of my mind. If the focus of my interest were to change, there would be many other perceptions that I could allow into my consciousness and many other activities that I could engage in with interest, even just whilst sitting here.

Thus what I am conscious of in the present relates to the matter I have in hand at the moment. My desire, my will, my active interest and my mind are focussed, and irrelevant sensations and ideas are filtered out. So the word "consciousness" in reality describes attention focussed on my immediate interest, and reflecting upon past experience so as to make sense of what I am doing.

I dwell in a field of concern that involves other people. This writing is for other people to read. It comes from my intimate professional involvement with other people's distress over many years. I have negotiated space for myself, in relation to other people, where I may work and write. My interest and behaviour are governed by my taking responsibility for what I am doing and being accountable to my family, community and God. So my conscious awareness enables me to find my way with what involves and interests me. It causes me to make credible sense of what I do, to give it meaning, and to develop understanding, so as to be able to give a satisfactory account.

By the grace of God, both self-control and language, and other creative talents, are available to me. I use them to make some of the fruits of my interests known, and to receive responses from others. But until I shall have become accustomed to the peace of true godliness in every aspect of my being (Hebrews 3:7 – 4:13), the account I owe to God and to mankind will inevitably be imperfect and therefore will cause me, and others, some anxiety and stress which may, regrettably, sometimes both distort my perception and also distort what I do. In other words, I may get it wrong sometimes. But the more I allow God to speak to me and heal me, the more godly, the more right with God, my conscience will become as it checks me to keep me on the narrow path of life.

The censor guards the heart

The mechanism involved in focussing my consciousness, and filtering out unnecessary material, is responsive to my past and present relationships, healed and unhealed. Most significantly it is responsive to my relationships with people and my relationship with God (Deuteronomy 4:24). These relationships determine what is acceptable, what sensory information I shall make sense of, and what is credible. And social concerns and anxieties, both past and present, dictate to a major extent what I perceive and give my attention to. What I call the "censor" is the mechanism that cuts out from awareness anything irrelevant, anything I cannot easily connect with, anything too much to comprehend or anything overwhelming in the circumstances. Thus the censor is the natural mechanism for guarding the heart (as in Proverbs 4:23 and 22:5).

Both the material that I have read concerning this subject I have in hand, and also many other things, like my current worries, or details of the news on the radio, or the contents of my drawer, or my recent conversation with my wife, are all readily available for my use. They easily enter my conscious awareness if there is the slightest hint that they may be relevant. It seems reasonable therefore to say they are "subconscious" – just below the surface of actual consciousness. And I am aware that subconscious material may influence what I write, sometimes without my being immediately aware of it. But this is monitored automatically. I trust my conscience under the guidance of the Holy Spirit to check me if undue prejudice, bias or irrelevance distorts what I do.

After all, there are all sorts of things, such as memories, speculations and emotions, that can come into your mind and be thought about if you have the mind to think about them. But for most of the time most of everything that is not relevant remains inaccessible to immediate consciousness. That is, it is in the 'unconscious', as they say. It is only brought to mind when needed - and sometimes with difficulty.

What actually appears in the mind at any given moment is determined by the relationships you have, including your relationship with God and your relationship, if any, with demons, and the events that are occurring. What comes to mind is also determined by memory, including memory that may be unhealed, censored and hidden so that it does not readily become conscious.

Although a memory may be triggered by some event, the censor will prevent the godly truth of that memory from coming into consciousness if it would be overwhelming in the circumstances. But the resultant tension can then cause truth to be distorted and inadvertent mistakes to be made.

God knows all things (1 John 3:20b) and he makes some of his knowledge accessible to the human race, according to his will (Deuteronomy 29:29). Those people who have found God's healing for past experience will have a relatively unimpeded relationship with the Holy Spirit and will be able to interpret their experience more truthfully, and also have a better knowledge of the mind of God, than people who do not have the Holy Spirit (1 Corinthians 2:6-16). Their experience will be interpreted soundly, giving them freedom and security in their being, so that their life is founded on a rock, as it were (Matthew 7:25). This makes for peace in spirit, soul and body no matter what befalls us (Psalm 46).

No one is perfect, however, and no one's sight is completely clear. Even people baptised in Holy Spirit have to contend with what gets in the way of experiencing the fullness of God's truth (John 16:33b). From God's perspective, the knowledge available to human beings, even those who wholeheartedly follow Jesus in the power of the Holy Spirit, is limited (Genesis 3:22-24). The human race lost their intimate, good, right, delightful, truthful, obedient relationship with God through disobedience following Satan's deception. God even confused our language so that the hubris of fallen humanity would be curtailed (Genesis 11:7). Those who have made Jesus their saviour and lord may know a foretaste of intimacy with God (Ephesians 1:14) but even they shall only fully regain such intimacy after passing through death. There are limitations on Christians' access to God until that day when "the dead will be raised imperishable" (1 Corinthians 15: 35-58).

Nevertheless, people who walk with the Lord receive guidance and revelation from him all the time, even in the most mundane situations. Consequently followers of Jesus Christ do not think in the same way as people who do not know him. Their language may be different and their understanding of suffering and adversity may be different. Sadly, however, the Christian way of thinking is no longer common or even acceptable in academic institutions. So secular professional qualifications can never be any guarantee of godly understanding. Academia justifies the world whilst the true church interprets the word of God. The differences are growing wider and deeper.

Occasionally those who love the Lord may actually be carried away into ecstasy by Holy Spirit, and receive wonderful revelation, whilst remaining in the body in this world (like Paul in 2 Corinthians 12:1-5). There are many instances of this sort of experience in both the Old and New Testaments and there are many people who have had such experiences since the Bible was written. However, there are other spirits, too, that can carry us away if we are so careless as to give them access to our souls. They put their hooks into the unwary, whether they be Christian or not; and they can speak to us insidiously, too. This is why God has made us with a guard for the heart, which I have called the censor, and why he gives spiritual discernment to those who love him.

The Bible says that those who have received the Holy Spirit have the mind of Christ (1 Corinthians 2:16) and can test and approve what God's will is. The Bible recommends that we test the spiritual forces that are active in any given situation to see whether or not they are from God. In 1 John 4:2 it says, "Every spirit that acknowledges that Jesus Christ has come in the flesh is from God but every spirit that does not acknowledge Jesus is not from God." And in 1 Corinthians 12:3 it says, "No man can say that Jesus is the Lord but by the Holy Ghost" (King James Version).

The censor needs healing

Everyone remains liable to disobedience, however, including every Christian (Romans 11:32-12:2). Therefore it behoves us both to know the word of God and also to be alert to the activity and prompting of the Holy Spirit (Matthew 25:1-13), always seeking our own healing from God. In this world there are a multitude of troubles to distract us and divert us from the will of God. Unless we deal with them all through the Lord Jesus by taking every thought captive for Christ we are liable to be deceived (2 Corinthians 10:5, John 16:13). The reality of this can sometimes be difficult and painful and we usually need the help of others, particularly their honesty, in order to help our censor to work according to the will of God.

Not only are there troubles in the outside world that we cannot understand or that may overwhelm us but there are also troubles within our own souls, from experiences for which we have been unable to find peace and healing. Past experience that has not been healed by God is liable to continue to cause hidden stress and anxiety. If the sense that has been made of past experience proves insufficient for it to be used again freely in the Lord's will, similar future events will not be handled well. Distortions of perception, and emotional reactions, can create prejudices that distort meaning and memory, which affect present behaviour and cause it to be inappropriate. Hitches like this can also prevent people from gleaning godly wisdom from people of past generations, by interfering with their discernment. But God wants to "turn the hearts of the fathers to their children and the hearts of the children to their fathers" (Malachi 4:6) by healing the memory and all the record, and making his truth known so that his people will act on it.[5]

Whenever events threaten to be overwhelming, their inward digestion is hindered. So full understanding is censored from consciousness, until sufficient sense can be made of those events to prevent embarrassing malfunction of the personality. The censor cuts out from consciousness whatever is too much. This is an automatic reaction of the living human body, which serves to protect the person.

God's word says, "I can do everything through him who gives me strength" (Philippians 4:13). Yet if the person has a lot of distorted perception or traumatic experience that has not been reconciled to God and remains unhealed, they cannot accept and receive the strength God makes available for them because it is sapped by the hidden stresses of their flesh.

They may be so used to living with this sort of stress, and the sickness that so often accompanies it, however, that these impediments will have become accepted as part of the personality and are not perceived as being of any particular bother, or in any need of healing.

We naturally make the best sense we can of experience, in order to give ourselves a modicum of peace. But our

---

[5] It is noteworthy in this respect that whilst those elders remained alive who had experienced everything the Lord had done in bringing Israel out of Egypt, Israel faithfully served the Lord (Joshua 24:31) but after those elders died their knowledge and wisdom were lost, and in consequence Israel got into serious difficulties. Experience of God's work in our lives provides a firm foundation (see Hebrews 10:35 – 11:1) but until the godly experience of previous generations, too, has been inwardly digested we remain unhealed (note Hebrews 13:17).

understanding may be deficient in consequence because, perhaps unwittingly, we have been resisting the work of the Holy Spirit so that our peace with God is not complete. Holy Spirit can shed his light and truth into all the various aspects of our being and bring God's healing and peace. Refusal to turn to God for healing is the cause of so very much trouble. All we need to do is allow him into our lives.

The subtle personal stresses created by avoided truths can be the cause of all sorts of distress and illness, including social problems and mental illness. After all, we are made in the image of God. Everything, past and present, can be reconciled to him. Then we shall know his peace in spirit, soul and body (2 Corinthians 7:1, 1 Thessalonians 5:23).

Lack of peace diverts us

The stresses and anxieties that divert us from God will also affect our choice of interest and our interpretation of events. They will have an influence on what is filtered out of conscious awareness, because we shall automatically censor memories that provoke excessive anxiety and confuse us. This occurs automatically so that we can keep on doing the work that needs to be done, and in order to avoid social discomfort or embarrassment.

The truth about them cannot be brought to God for complete healing unless there is sufficient safety, time and space to consider everything with him. God's power is made perfect in weakness (2 Corinthians 12:9) and it has to be safe in order to be weak. Only when the person has come to the right time and place, and is ready, does the Holy Spirit bring to light what needs to be healed.

Repetition compulsion

If any attempt is made to focus on issues that remind the person of unresolved trouble and unhealed experience when the time and place are wrong or when the person is not ready, there will immediately be too much stress to consider the full truth of it, and God's peace will, often in some very plausible way, be missed.

Yet whilst the true but unhealed memory is unavailable for recall into consciousness, issues that threaten to trigger that memory will inevitably recur. They will crop up unexpectedly in that person's life, creating anxiety and difficulties and influencing what the person does and does not do, and distorting godly judgement about issues in any way related to the unhealed experience.

Childhood trauma

Thus, for example, a Christian man whose parents had insisted, when he was a child, that little children should be seen and not heard, was brutal towards his grandchildren if they cried, without really understanding how or why he was wounding them. He also suffered high blood pressure and dizziness. He only repented of his behaviour after visiting his doctor, who warned him of the risks of having a stroke. Only then did he find the sense to seek the Lord for healing. Soon after, as he was talking with his family, he remembered the frustrations and pain of his childhood, and was able to forgive, and be free of his bitterness and the baleful effects in his body.

There will be a partial cut-off from God's truth, an inability to receive his full revelation of truth about events, until the Lord's healing begins to be received. Into that cut-off, deceptions and demons may readily have moved to distort the way the mind is made up, and to make that person's behaviour difficult, just as a demon of cruelty attached itself to that man's childhood wounds.

Thus the censor that controls the person's focus of attention will be distorted, just as that man was oversensitive to children's tears. Perception will be distorted, and the true cause of the inner stress and the lack of godly peace may remain unknown, until the Holy Spirit reveals the relevant memory in the light of God's presence. Then it can be yielded to God through Jesus, who took it on the cross. Then our Father will heal the details.[6]

Overwhelming experience before the age of about eight is not usually processed in a mature adult way. Until that sort of age a child uncritically accepts the judgements of parents. Violence, cruelty and neglect are surprisingly common, so too is the worship of deities that fail to bring peace, kindness, goodness and faithful love. A child who has experienced manipulation, deception and cruelty before the age of eight or so, will have accepted it as a normal part of life, so the trauma will be hidden more deeply. And a significant amount of the trauma to which children are exposed is sexual. Most abuse comes from people the child knows and it frequently goes unacknowledged and unpunished, because the standards by which evidence is usually judged in courts of law belong to this world, so evidence is often successfully disputed.

Parents or carers may enable the child to find healing by allowing the child to tell what happened through play and drawing, by containing the situation and not abandoning the process, and by not trying too hard to understand everything all at once or asking too many questions, and through prayer to Almighty God, and allowing God to take his time with the child.

If there are overwhelming experiences that remain unhealed they may cause a young child to begin to behave in odd ways in order to prevent traumatic memory re-surfacing. Then as the child grows up the personality and behaviour, even the thoughts and memories, may become different in different situations. The personality may therefore seem to some extent or other to be changeable and fragmented. There is no wholeness because the person cannot afford the automatic connection with particular

---

[6] You will not be truly healed by imagining Jesus providing a better experience, as some people try to do, but by God's presence, in the present, healing you of the wounds you actually received, and the associated sins, bondages and unclean spirits, and through allowing the Holy Spirit to renew your mind so that you see things God's way.

memories for fear of re-living them without any credible prospect of healing being manageable.

Some people who have been tortured and whose lives have been seriously threatened, furthermore, may fear the possible consequences of bringing the facts to light. When this happens to adults they will commonly just not go there. They will develop an automatic ability to block any prospect of those events coming in to consciousness or being spoken about. Inevitably this will affect their behaviour and make them hard of heart.

Seriously distressing experiences often cannot be wholly remembered. So those experiences will not be fully integrated into intelligent adult behaviour. They will not have been healed and transformed by the Lord into softening the heart and into compassion. This is common. And it involves not only extreme situations but also all unhealed deception and accusation and distortion of godly truth.

Commonly, therefore, when the child grows up behaviour will not be totally consistent. Powerful emotions and reactions may appear that seem inappropriate. This may even destroy relationships. There may also be particular learning difficulties. There may even be unexpectedly disturbing occasions when events from the past seem to be re-lived, or almost re-lived.

Sometimes the person may seem to be back in an old scenario, or may wander off in a fugue not knowing where they are going or why they should suddenly be automatically avoiding reality. Flashback memories may recur, or nightmares, seeming to put the person suddenly right back in shock and trauma. Sometimes unarticulated emotions from trauma, rejection, or deception, that have been stored hidden in the memory, may cause panic, or be very confusing. Sometimes the person may seem to behave in an odd manner because they are being reminded of what has hitherto been inexpressible.

Strange behaviour may be an attempt both to give expression to the distress of the memory and also to prevent apparent disintegration of the mind, which can be experienced as a sort of death or a terrible fear of death - the person may feel depersonalised, petrified, in pieces or even effectively obliterated. This sort of event is further discussed in Chapter 8.

Full healing only comes after the Holy Spirit reveals what needs to be recalled and remembered for the experience to be reconciled to God through our Lord Jesus. This is a process that takes time – often quite a long time.

Ontological insecurity

It is in childhood that the intensity of learning is greatest. And if there should be a significant amount of unhealed, deceptively perceived experience not only from earliest childhood but also inherited through parents and prevalent in the culture, it will be the cause of deep-seated insecurity in the person's very being. Some philosophers have usefully termed this 'ontological insecurity'.[7]

Until there is healing, it will affect both the development of understanding and also the emotional and behavioural responses to many, various situations. If circumstances are such that the person comes to psychiatric attention, this ontological insecurity may contribute to a diagnosis of 'personality-disorder', 'depression', or 'schizophrenia.'

Of course healing can come through accepting the Lord Jesus as saviour, and really getting to know God, in whose image we are made, and finding his peace for spirit, soul and body. Frequently this will be a process that takes time, although a very rapid transformation does seem to occur in some people as they become baptised in Holy Spirit.

---

[7] Kierkegaard in *The Concept of Anxiety (1844)*, etc., Tillich in *The Courage to Be (1952)* and in *Biblical Religion and the Search for Ultimate Reality (1955)* etc., and Niebuhr in *Experiential* in Chapters 5 and 8.*Religion (1972)* etc., have described this as a root of sinful behaviour. This is further discussed in Chapters 5 and 8.

Healing for torment

If at any age a person's experiences should be utterly shattering, the overwhelming details may be largely censored out of mind. This is natural. It may occur after accidents or violent assaults, or abuse, or horrific battle, or any other trauma, mental, emotional or physical. Rape can be like this. If memory is persistently tormenting, recall may sometimes be incomplete. The whole experience may be too stupendous or too horrendous to be allowed into full consciousness with all the implications.

Although you may try to put the torment out of your mind, sooner or later, for the sake of your own health, some healing may seem necessary. Being reconciled to God about it may seem impossible.

But this would not mean accepting it. God knows what happened. Even though you may not have had his protection at the time it occurred, he will heal you. If you turn to him he will accept you because he loves you. Receiving his healing involves allowing the loving person of God to be present for you, and permitting Jesus to take your trauma, casting it on him (1 Peter 5:7). Jesus died on a cross for the sins of the whole world. He overcame all that evil. He overcame the powers of Satan and death and destruction, and he rose from the dead.

Find a safe place. Then yield to Jesus the emotion, the horror, the brutality, the hate, the rage, the violence, the fear, the false guilt that so often accompanies victimhood, the dirt, the shame, the wounds, and all the personal contamination of the attacker. God enabled his only begotten Son Jesus to take it all on the cross for you. Therefore allow him to do so (read Isaiah 53:4-5; Matthew 8:17; Matthew 11:28; 1 Peter 2:24).

If the intense emotion persists, you may need to expel a demon. Confess the thought or emotion, renounce the demon and command it out in the name of Jesus. It usually comes out in a cough or vomit. Receive the Lord's forgiveness and healing. Then when eventually you are ready to do so, thank him with all your heart and mind. Receive his comfort and allow his blood to purify you (1 John 1:7). Let him make you whole again. This may take some time.[8]

Censorship of bodily memory

Without Jesus, all the emotion could drive you out of your mind. It may be too much to articulate. Its expression could re-traumatize you and change you as a person by leaving, as it were, an ulcer of madness within your soul so that your mind would be unstable and your behaviour unpredictable. There could be all sorts of fears and dreads and all sorts of bitterness, sensitivities and nightmares. You could feel unworthy in some way. You might compensate for these attitudes by behaving in ways that could cause you further harm, without really knowing why. Trauma, loss, torture, domination, and early rejection, deception and alienation, can leave deep unconscious memory wounds that continue to threaten inner security and distort perception, judgement and behaviour.

Furthermore, elements of the personality or of the living body, or both, may occasionally be sacrificed (in other words censored out of action and devoted to inaction) in order to retain sufficient cohesion of the personality to enable the person to function in this world despite the wounds. Memory resides in our bodies. Jesus recognises that this is part of the human condition when he says, "...if your eye causes you to sin, pluck it out." (Mark 9:47). The

---

[8] Whether or not experience is actually recalled, the way in which it may be recalled is a function not only of the extent of the past trauma, of the confusion, and of the measure of God's grace, but also of the degree of acceptance by present hearers. A traumatized person will have no natural desire to be re-traumatized by the misunderstanding of others, nor to be overwhelmed again by their own emotion and pain. The process of healing is usually gentle and gradual, and it may be best to bind up all the demons that may be attached to emotions and to minister the Lord's healing to the trauma, then deal with the rest at the right moment. And although a measure of God's healing may come without full recall, I do not believe experience can be said to be fully healed until it can, one day, be addressed consciously and with forgiveness.

"eye" may be put out of action, one way or another, if it should seem that trouble and conflict related to the "eye" cannot be healed.

Parts of the living soul or body, or both, may be automatically plucked out, dispensed with, and not brought into action in some way, by people who have not found God's full healing, and whose focus has had to be on survival in this world. This even happened to Paul, who lost his sight for three days until he received God's healing in the name of Jesus through Ananias (Acts 9). In the same way, a person may lose the use of an arm, or of the memory, or of some other part of the body or soul, in order to cope with hidden inner turmoil until healing can be received.

Protective defence mechanisms, including those described in psychological textbooks, may censor elements of perception, memory recall, cognition, imagination, the use of language, or of parts of the body, in order to prevent potentially overwhelming aspects of experience from being known or disastrously acted upon. All this is discussed more particularly in Chapter 7, but it applies to the other chapters of this book, too.

Thus breakdowns and dissociative splits both in the manifestation of personality, and also in the function of the living body, may become apparent due to the activity of the censor in an unhealed person. Although these are often well camouflaged, they are the roots of illness. They may be excused, of course, and thus discounted, through being given an authoritative medical diagnosis.

Breakdown

A moment of tragedy may arrive when current stress and inner anxiety are so great that the person no longer copes. The censor is overridden. Breakdown is often immediately preceded by a heightened intensity of awareness or a powerful sense of unreality, which are signs that the censor in the soul is totally over-stressed, like a fuse about to blow. Then the attention may be displaced either into irrelevant obsessive activity that avoids the issue, or into generalised, unfocussed anxiety. Panic may become overwhelming. Or there may be confusion and double-mindedness. Or there may be out-of-body experiences or other dissociation. Both hope and focus may be jettisoned, and the will may thus be stymied. Attention may then drift in any direction, sometimes with grossly exuberant reactions and emotions. People in this sort of condition may sometimes become a dangerous threat to other people, and they are then liable to be restrained, controlled, and diagnosed by psychiatrists.

This sort of tragedy could be prevented by the healing activity of people who belong in the kingdom of God. Being salt and light in this world (Matthew 5:13-14) involves speaking words "full of grace, seasoned with salt" (Colossians 4:6). Jesus said, "For where two or three come together into my name, there am I with them" (Matthew 18:20). The person of the Lord Jesus revealed through his people, like this, is a healing presence. It becomes safe for truth to come into the light. Comfort is ministered to the soul. Miracles occur.

Salt and light

The Holy Bible provides adequate understanding for such ministry, but the discipline of theology has been too worldly. Our understanding has consequently been distorted. Let us therefore recapitulate and apply the living teaching of Jesus more specifically.

Much of the unhealed past experience that is censored, so that our focus of interest and activity is distorted in this way by what is happening in the present, comes from wounds that were inflicted on us in the past by others. But, since our human nature is fallen, our natural responses to those wounds will have been sinful. So we shall have been hurt not only by old wounds by our own reactive sin, too.

Bad experiences naturally cause bad reactions that develop into bad habits. People may lie to us and steal from us. They may misunderstand and reject us. They may wrongly accuse and abuse us. All this may get worse if we react to them badly.

Moreover, we may actually believe their judgements and their deceptions. We may even believe ourselves to be in the wrong. We may even count ourselves worthless in consequence. And we may justify our misperceptions and misunderstandings and, in consequence, wound many others. We may fail to realise why we are so confused and despondent, and why we feel so rejected, and prefer to accept a psychiatric diagnosis because we have found no faith for any other way of thinking. So in God's eyes we may eventually have believed so much untruth that the operation of our minds has become grossly distorted. We shall have trusted our natural reactions and believed other people in preference to allowing God's light to penetrate our understanding.

But unhealed experience is unfinished business with God. And it may accumulate down the generations, and be inherited, so that a person may say, for example, "My father used to get depressed in the same way I do." So there is an insecurity in every one of us until both our own experience and also the iniquity inherited from our ancestors are made right with God, through the blood of Jesus, and healed.

We can accept with thankful hearts that the blood of the Lord Jesus was shed to redeem us from our fallen human nature. Then we can confess our sin to God and he will forgive our sin and take away our guilt and shame. We can pray to God and forgive our ancestors, and we can be forgiven for the sin we carry in us from them. And we can ask him to break the power of wrong influences from our ancestors. And we can expel inherited demons, and all the demons we have otherwise acquired, in the name of Jesus. Then we must listen to that still, small voice who speaks truth.

As we consider how the censor in our souls has been affected by our sin, and by Satan, we may realise that God's words to Isaiah, recorded in Chapter 6, verses 9 and 10, are very relevant to the development of mental illness: "He said, 'Go and tell this people: "You will be ever hearing, but never understanding; you will be ever seeing but never perceiving. This people's heart has become calloused; they hardly hear with their ears and they have closed their eyes. Otherwise they might see with their eyes, hear with their ears, understand with their hearts and turn and be healed."'"(Isaiah 6:9-10, Septuagint).

What is it, according to The Holy Bible, that hardens the heart, dulls the ears and closes the eyes to the experience of the truth of God? What is it that censors our understanding and perception and filters out issues we cannot handle? And what is the remedy?

Isaiah was given the answer (whether he consciously knew the full implication or not) when he wrote a little later, in Chapter 7:13-14: "Hear now, you house of David! Is it not enough to try the patience of men? Will you try the patience of God also? Therefore the Lord himself will give you a sign: The virgin will be with child and will give birth to a son, and they will call him Immanuel." And in Chapter 9 Isaiah wrote that a great light from God would dawn upon people walking in darkness through a child from God who would be born amongst his people Israel.

That child was the Lord Jesus, Mashiach of the Jews who, when he grew to manhood, told the parable of the sower: ""Listen! A farmer went out to sow his seed. As he was scattering his seed, some fell along the path and the birds came and ate it up. Some fell on rocky places where it did not have much soil. It sprang up quickly, because the soil was shallow. But when the sun came up, the plants were scorched, and they withered because they had no root. Other seed fell among thorns, which grew up and choked the plants, so that they did not bear grain. Still other seed fell on good soil. It came up, grew and produced a crop, multiplying thirty, sixty or even a hundred times." Then Jesus said, "He who has ears to hear, let him hear."" (Mark 4:3-9).

When Jesus interpreted this parable to his disciples he taught that some people's inability to understand and perceive truthfully, is caused by the snares of Satan and his "birds."[9] Jesus told elsewhere how Satan is a thief, a destroyer and a murderer (John 10:10). Revelation 12:9-10 explains that Satan operates through accusation and deception. Satan's terrors often stop people's ears and eyes through fear, seduction and confusion. All sorts of distortions of God's truth operate to mislead us along our path in this world. But in John 8:47 Jesus says, "He who belongs to God hears what God says".

Now, we belong to God when we accept Jesus (John 1:12-13). God cares for his people and longs for them to hear his voice (John 10:1-21) but those who do not receive Jesus, and therefore do not belong to God, belong within Satan's domain, whether they know it or not, and may not hear God so well (John 8: 42-47). God's words for them will be more effectively censored because they cannot be fully healed until they come to Jesus.

Jesus' interpretation of his parable can also be seen to describe how some people may hear and receive God's truth with joy but then lose it because unhealed, rocky places in their souls prevent them from fully accepting it so as to develop a root of understanding that holds good through times of trouble or persecution.

Other people, of course, allow his truth to be choked by worries, or by the deceitful pleasures of this world. In other words, understanding is quenched when they allow themselves to be distracted. And this will more readily occur when there are unhealed, resistant and well-defended wounds in the soul with consequent sins and deceptive habits of mind.

Good soil, which allows the root to grow deep and produce a harvest, comes from hearing God's word, even in difficult circumstances, accepting it, considering it carefully, repenting, understanding, receiving the Lord's healing and guidance, and

---

[9] Compare Genesis 15:11. The "birds" in both cases are demons.

being encouraged with the faith that fills the heart with peace and joy for obedience to him.

By the grace of God people who know such healing experience will cause both faith and the harvest to increase (Mark 4:1-29).

Human beings of Adam's race lost their godly innocence when, tempted by Satan, he and his wife Eve allowed doubt about God's word to come into their hearts (Genesis 3:1). From then on we have generally failed to hear him clearly and, consequently, when times of trouble have come upon us our fallen nature turns away from him. In periods of anxiety and torment our natural instincts and unregenerate reasoning have too often been what has driven our feelings and thoughts and behaviour. We should have listened to our Father God instead, who created us in his image and who loves us and desires to save us!

Jesus also tells us that those who have been forgiven more will love him more (Luke 7:36-50) and Peter says that whoever has suffered in his body with Jesus is done with sin (1 Peter 4:1). Paul urges us to develop godly character through persevering in the Lord when we suffer (Romans 5:1-5). Therefore, I conclude that the root of understanding that Jesus described will grow through repentance, through yielding our sufferings to him and seeking his forgiveness, his healing, his revelation and his guidance. Some would describe this as a process of 'working through' all our difficulties and confusions with Jesus. Others would call it a process of sanctification. This way, all that has been in the dark, excluded from conscious awareness, may become apparent. And as it comes into the light we can receive God's healing (John 1:4-9, John 3:21, 1 John 1:5-7).

Jesus advises us to be careful how we listen, "for there is nothing hidden that will not be disclosed" (Luke 8:17) and "with the measure you use it will be measured to you, and even more" (Mark 5:24). So he is speaking of receiving his Spirit, his new life, and his revelations and words, so that our hearts understand our experience, and our eyes and ears open with his truth to perceive

44

his way. When we receive the Holy Spirit, the mechanism within the soul that controls what we allow into our conscious awareness, which I have called the censor, changes so that we may have eyes to see and ears to hear and hearts to understand. In God's timing, and under his direction, stress and anxiety can depart and his truth and peace can be received with healing. Yet he never overrides our free will[10] and we can always refuse to accept his revelation. If we refuse him, however, our root of understanding will not grow, and therefore we shall not bear so much of his fruit.

Jesus says, "I am the way and the truth and the life. No-one comes to the Father except through me." (John 14:6). We may regain a living relationship with God through Jesus his only begotten Son, who was crucified to redeem us and rose from the dead the third day after, and whose blood was shed to make atonement for us. Thus Isaiah's prophecy is fulfilled and Immanuel opens our ears and our eyes, and softens our hearts so that they may become like the hearts of little children, responding to our Father without guile (Matthew 19: 13-15, Mark 10:13-16, Luke 18:15-17, John 1:47). Jesus heals the censor so that we may find the way and the truth and abundant, eternal life.

Thus the processes of repentance, of forgiving, of renewing the mind (Romans 12:2), of seeking holiness (Hebrews 12:10-14), of casting our cares on him (1Peter 5:7) as we suffer in this fallen world (John 16:33, 2 Corinthians 7:10, 1 Peter 4:1), are a processes of overcoming our sinful nature and getting rid of the guile and iniquity that get in the way of a good relationship with our Father God. He abounds in mercy! His love endures for ever (Psalm 103)! This is the only truly effective process for healing the mind, the soul, the body, and all our relationships.

---

[10] On those occasions when he may seem to be overriding our free will we may discover that he has actually been drawing us to a point where he can successfully challenge our stubbornness (e.g. the conversion of Paul – see Chapter 10).

Iniquity comes from our natural reactions to our experiences, from our wilful sin and from the experiences and sin of our ancestors. But every experience of life can be made right with God and healed, so that we actually perceive with his ears and eyes and heart, his way.

Thus wounds of the soul caused by violence, loss, domination, curses and false accusation, and so on, may be healed through Jesus. We may be relieved of ungodly desires and worries and set free from sinful habits. Relationships that are wrong with God may be put right and their effects may be healed. We may be delivered from unclean spirits. We can be cleansed of inherited iniquity. Confusion, perplexity and bewilderment may be clarified truthfully, and the deceptions of Satan revealed, as the Holy Spirit dispels the darkness.

All these are causes of mental illness. We can be driven out of our minds by experience that is censored out of mind unhealed. But until we are set free by the power of the Holy Spirit and allow him to transform our lives, the censor guards the heart and mind according to the dictates of our fallen human nature.

No matter how unspeakable, terrible or confused our past experience may have been, no matter how many the lies, no matter how deep the guilt or how hopeless the situation may seem, through the power of the Holy Spirit the love of God can be made manifest to overcome bitterness and fear (1 John 4:18) and to hold the person safe (Psalm 31:20) whilst memory is healed and whilst the truth of God is revealed and forgiveness becomes possible. Demons then have to depart. The censor is healed and enables the person to focus unimpeded on God's truth and God's will (2 Corinthians 3:16). Then by the grace of God the censor is no longer distorted by always having to keep out of conscious awareness material that causes constant stress and threatens to undermine health and destroy sanity.

Until the censor is healed by the Lord it veils the truth (2 Corinthians 4:3-4) and keeps us focussed on this world for our security. Behind its veil we try to hide away from the glory of

God with our fallen sensitivities and senselessness, and with our faithlessness, shame, heartlessness and ruthlessness (Romans 1:31, Genesis 3:8). In this veiled state the Bible says we are asleep with a spirit of stupor (Romans 11:8, Deuteronomy 29:4, Isaiah 29:10) from which the Lord bids us, 'Wake up!' (Isaiah 51:9 ff. and Ephesians 5:14). The person behind the blinding of our minds is Satan, the Prince of this world (2 Corinthians 4:4), whom the Lord Jesus overcame when he died on a cross and rose from the dead the third day. Because of Jesus, the almighty majesty of God is no longer unapproachable for us or veiled (Luke 23:45). Because of what Jesus accomplished on the cross we may enter God's presence and receive his healing.

Through allowing Jesus to remove the veil with love (Song of Songs 1:7, 2:14 and 4:1 – 5:1), you may know your redeemer and allow him into yourself to live in you. Then it becomes possible for all your experience, your soul, your body, and your relationships, to be healed and transformed. All the true reality of your person, the person God made you to be, may then willingly be yielded to him and live freely in this world in his love.

This way we become equipped and perfected for the place he has for us (2 Timothy 3:16-17 KJV). He is our light and our salvation (Psalm 27:1). He has the words of eternal life.

47

3

TRANCE

We have seen that the censor, the mechanism within the soul that controls what we allow into our personal conscious awareness, both focuses attention on our interest and also guards the heart and mind from being overwhelmed.

Mothers' influence

Even from the very earliest moments of life the censor learns by trial and error to protect the person from being overwhelmed. Implanted in the mother's womb, the child is relatively protected from the effects of the mother's everyday emotions through being surrounded by amniotic fluid and by not having the same blood circulation. Even if the mother suffers severe physical shocks, the baby usually has priority protection and survives quite easily. However, the spiritual influences in the mother's life, her attitudes, including the unhealed experiences of her own life, affect the child much more than shock, and these become built into the child's censor. The extent of the mother's lack of healing often becomes manifest in the child later, as unhealed inherited attitudes. Particular traits of personality develop from background parental influences. They naturally affect the direction of later interests and fascinations.

After the child is born and begins to suckle at the mother's breast, the child may fall asleep only to waken sufficiently to suck a little more. Protected by the mother's love and concern, and in complete trust, developing defences are lulled by sleep; yet the child's attention remains focussed enough to suck periodically if the teat comes into the mouth. Even if there should be quite a lot of disturbance, the child will still sleep and occasionally suck on the teat provided the mother herself does not become too upset.

The spirit of the mother profoundly affects the child during those moments.[11] And through touch, through feeding, through eye contact, and through acceptance of the child's excreta and mess, the mother's loving affirmation of the child's identity tells the child, "You belong! I see you! We love you!" And she encourages the child to thrive. Even if feeding should be accompanied by serious distress and emotional turbulence, the child would still be likely to thrive. Whatever is not relevant to survival will be cut out from the child's immediate attention by the child's automatic censorship mechanism. In Chapter 5 of *Healing for the Wounded Life,* however, I have described how memory of emotional wounds and distresses sustained during this period can actually be manifest later as unhealed experience, although the child will probably thrive nevertheless.

The power of entrancement and hypnosis

When a little older, the child may sit on the mother's knee and fall asleep whilst listening to an enchanting bedtime story. Although apparently asleep, the child may not only remember the story but also be quite deeply affected by it, particularly if the story is told with loving authority and seems connected with feelings relevant to everyday events. The child may be especially enchanted if the meaning of the story gives significance to deep issues currently being resolved such as, for example, "What is bad?" "I am angry!" "What is dangerous?" and "I am frightened of that man." Stories may help the child make sense of the world, find healing for wounds and develop understanding.

Still later in life, an adult person can be lulled into the same sort of trance by the soothingly authoritative voice of a hypnotist as the attention of the eyes is focussed, for example, on his

---

[11] Lion cubs fail to learn to hunt and kill aggressively if they do not feed from the teat of their mother!

pocket-watch slowly swinging to and fro. A partial inhibition occurs of the natural adult defences that guard heart and mind. The censorship mechanism is rendered sufficiently defenceless for the person to go partly to sleep, like a baby with its mother only this time under the supposedly benign influence of the hypnotist. It is then possible for the hypnotist to make suggestions and make the person do things that would not otherwise be accepted. The will becomes biddable and willing.

I do not recommend anyone to submit to being manipulated in this way but I am using this example to show how attention may be given trustingly, unguardedly and passively, just as a child is enchanted by the mother's story, to interesting things that seem to offer some sort of release or comfort for latent dissatisfaction and stress. The censor does not guard against such deception unless taught credibly how to do so (Hebrews 5:14).

Entranced may mean demonic entrance

Just as attention was unwittingly captured by the watch swinging to and fro, in order to enable the hypnotist to gain access to a person's heart and mind, so we too can be subliminally manipulated through allowing ourselves to be lulled to sleep about issues we would rather not think about. Matters which seem impossible to resolve in the time available, or because they actually distress us too much, or because they seem potentially overwhelming, are readily censored out of mind. But the feelings and emotions connected with them remain latent within us and can be harnessed by manipulators. We may be asleep to some things that are important for us although we may be alert to others. Thus it is possible for us to be seduced into being entranced and lulled into a false sense of security whilst unwittingly being dominated, manipulated and controlled.

The hypnotist will not, however, be so readily able to dominate people who are alert and walking clear with the Holy Spirit. People who have found God's healing for their own souls, and who continue to make their peace with God by speaking with him about everything that affects them, whether good or bad (2 Corinthians 10:3-5), will have developed discernment. The Holy Spirit will tell people who are walking clear like this what they need to know about what is really going on (1 Corinthians 2:15-16 and 2 Corinthians 9:8). Holy Spirit reveals fruitless deeds of darkness and what the disobedient do in secret (Ephesians 5:11-14, Good News Bible). Holy Spirit enables us to see how the world really is. And when we know the Father well enough we shall have sufficient discernment to be relatively protected from being deceived (Romans 10:11 & 13). To allow ourselves to become complacent, however, would be foolish. Should we discover we are falling into temptation, we can resist it firmly and command Satan away. We have authority to do this because belong to Jesus (Romans 6:11-13, James 4:7).

Satan's tricks

The Bible essentially describes two means of putting out of action the natural censorship mechanism that guards the heart and mind. The Holy Spirit revealed them to John, the writer of Revelation. They are deception and accusation, the two weapons of Satan (Revelation 12:9-10).

The shock and awe of accusation and violence can stun us and put our defences out of action as effectively as deception. But accusation can often be more subtle than that. Hindrances in our relationship with the Holy Spirit generate confusion, doubt and uncertainty about truth. In a state of doubt, anxiety or panic a person may take wrong direction and infer wrong meanings so as to become deceived. And when our mistakes are realised we may feel accused and become ashamed and guilty. If we have never known divine forgiveness we may then make the assumption that we are condemned (see Genesis 3). Then we may really feel rejected, and even abandon hope. We may feel lost and confused, and develop a fear of abandonment, of death and of judgement. As faith is lost, the only remnant of joy that remains will become fixed on the things of this world. The meaninglessness of the secular world without God will nevertheless eventually become apparent (as described in Ecclesiastes). When this happens it brings with it a rather dreadful feeling of emptiness and ennui.

As we lose God's protection, the accusations of Satan grow. We can become victims of curses, violence, cruel punishment, torment and suffering (described in Deuteronomy 28). Then a person without a sound personal relationship with God may grasp at straws or at anything that seems to make sense at the time. Both deception and accusation may thus override the defences of the censor and produce a sort of trance, an avoidance of true reality. Thus they lead a person astray by causing the person to hook into things and ideas that ultimately prove insubstantial. If the person caught in such deceptions becomes lost and confused and is then faced with further accusations and curses, he or she could even become quite psychotic. [12]

Unhealed personal issues can prevent us from addressing the full facts of reality soberly with God in sincerity and truth. The memory of unhealed experiences is held within us in a state of inhibition that affects the censor, making it repress any suggestion of a reminder of them, lest our peace be disturbed without there being any apparent remedy - as described in the previous chapter.

Dangers of fascination

It is the pent-up emotion and stress of coping with such unhealed issues, with thoughts not reconciled to God, that the tempter may offer to relieve through presenting the person with some tantalising object of fascination. Much of the sort of trouble that ensues may be avoided in childhood by having nothing to do with horror or magic or occultism or fairy tales, and sticking instead to sincerity and truth, and ordinary objects for play, and

---

[12] See footnote 70, in Chapter 8, on the "double bind."

by discussing everything openly with the child from the start, and keeping adventure real.

Children are particularly vulnerable to misleading enchantment both because they are more trusting and also because immature minds easily become fascinated. What fascinates a person is to some extent stimulating and exciting, a focus for enquiry and learning and emotional expression. But it is dangerous to assume simply that what is exciting is good because it keeps the children entertained. Children can be influenced easily in their thoughts and behaviour by being enticed and excited by teaching that is wrong with God, perpetrated by people who may not be intentionally malicious but who neither know nor respect the Lord Jesus. Many of the stories, films, amusements, toys and illustrations used to entertain and placate children are dangerous rubbish, serving only to help them avoid the truth of what is really going on by encouraging them to live in a virtual reality that can seduce them into dangerous pathways.

Encouraging children's natural resilience

When children accept Biblical truth about their most fundamental questions from loving parents, they tend to develop sound judgement and peace. Their most fundamental and significant issues generally relate to where things and people come from and go to, and death, and guilt, and meaning.[13] Therefore children need to be protected by parents at least until sufficient maturity has developed for the main ramifications of these questions to have been substantially answered.

By giving wise, biblically correct responses that interest them without exasperating them (Ephesians 6:4), children can gain sufficient understanding and wisdom from an early age to overcome the false accusations, deceptions and con-tricks of the world, the flesh and the devil as they grow up.

---

[13] Tillich, P. (1952) *The Courage to Be*, New Haven & London, Yale University Press.

Children are able to face true reality, no matter how terrible, provided the wool is not pulled over their eyes and provided they are loved unconditionally by their mothers and fathers. Children even of primary school age can develop the necessary caution and wisdom if the parents at home love Jesus, give time to their children, guide and encourage their play, have the courage to speak sincerely and truthfully about real issues, know how to apply the word of God, reject excitement and escapism and do not allow themselves to be too distracted by worry.

If every sort of issue that arises in the family is brought into the light and spoken about and laid before the Lord in the children's presence, discernment may be learned very early (Ephesians 5:1 - 6:4). But sadly too many parents have never faced basic facts of their own lives and are coping with many of their own unhealed wounds. Therefore, since the avoidance of fundamental issues is so very common, it is now necessary to discuss further how people may not only be led astray but may also become seriously mentally ill through becoming entranced, so that Christians may grasp how to tackle social problems.

Manipulation for radical change

Fascination with something that maintains a hold on the focus of attention may unwittingly allow powerful influences into the heart and mind. To achieve this, the fascination does not even need to be good or desirable. Sometimes what fascinates us may be religious. Often, however, it may be more morbid than it seems. People may be absolutely entranced by all sorts of fascinating spectacles they do not really understand.

Sometimes people are captivated whilst paralysed with confusion, shock or fear. They may subsequently find themselves unwittingly enslaved to something or other, or to someone, so that they become really quite obsessed. Pop idols trade on this, for example.

The person may be opened up in overwhelming situations that are quite enchanting but all together far too much completely to comprehend. All sorts of emotion will be stimulated. The process of being opened up in this way may quite violently call into question previously held assumptions, habits and beliefs, and leave the person feeling there is nothing to hold on to any more except the idol or the ideology the attention of the senses has become hypnotically focussed upon. It can be like going on a roller coaster for the first time and holding on to the rail to save oneself from a grim death. It may even cause some degree of mental breakdown, weeping, fainting, confusion or panic.

The person is fascinated and seduced, then made suggestible, and then manipulated to focus attention on what will apparently save them. The means of salvation is often represented as a charismatic person. Interest in the charismatic cause, in the conveyed message, will become obsessive almost inevitably, and will be adopted with religious fervour. And then the person can be further manipulated and controlled through that fascination.

The person becomes fascinated and seduced in this way when there emotional issues of deep significance in their lives for which they have not been able to find godly healing and peace. The object of fascination hooks into the person's unmitigated desires and needs. Thus by overwhelming the senses with shock and awe, and totally unnerving the individual, and then playing on unhealed issues about which freedom[14] has never been found because they have not been reconciled to God, the person is fed with ideas and influences that deceptively seem to promise plausible answers, some degree of satisfaction, pleasure or excitement, or even some divine purpose.

Then these new ideas and influences are built up, so that they, too, overload the mind and the heart. They would take a long time fully to understand. Meanwhile, however, representative logos and motifs, and charismatic people, reinforce the message so that full understanding never seems necessary, and the person

---

[14] Freedom involves healing.

decides to trust those with the plausible answers. So the politics, the religion or the product seem convincing, and the person loses autonomy, loses free will. The mechanism of censorship has been overcome, and becomes a willing pawn in the enslavement. This is sorcery

This is how Hitler rose to power. All aggressive war is engendered this way.

What do you do when you don't know what to do?

What if all you have hitherto believed in should eventually prove disappointing and worthless? You than find yourself in another state of more brutal mental breakdown! When a person can no longer hold the self together, or cope safely, and can find no one good enough really to help, that person may become suggestible, so that the focus of attention fixes on anything or anyone that may seem to offer some possibility of hope or relief. Old ways of making personal judgements and decisions may then be discarded and new beliefs adopted.

Unless the new ways are founded on the rock of Jesus, however, and relationship established with him so that the word of God may be believed, these new beliefs may be no better than the old.

There are many mistaken and unscrupulous people who, like Hitler, use such methods in order to manipulate and dominate other people for personal, religious or political ends that eventually prove disastrous. They play on people's weaknesses and stimulate their emotions to cause some degree of enchantment, or even breakdown, so that people change, and adopt the new ideas and ways that are offered.

Only when you are spiritually aware can you see that the people who do this sort of thing have actually invoked spiritual beings, gods, and demons whose spiritual power works through them to affect other people deeply, stirring up their emotions in particular ways, changing the way they make decisions and judgements and controlling what happens. People who succumb to this adopt the character of the spiritual beings involved, and become the means for spiritual principalities, powers and demons to achieve their goals.[15]

Soundness of mind

Every sort of mental breakdown may always be seen as a tragic result of a spiritual crisis in which the firm ground of God and his word have not been found, and in which the world, the flesh and the devil have combined to undermine personal freedom. And, frankly, no one is immune in this fallen world. But Jesus is Lord of lords and King of kings; and God has given disciples of Jesus - those individuals in whose hearts he reigns as king - his authority to overcome all the power of the enemy (Luke 10:18-20). And God, who has made mankind in his own image, bestows within them "the spirit...of power, and of love, and of a sound mind" (2 Timothy 1:7, KJV) which bears fruit for the kingdom if constantly fuelled by loving obedience to the living word of God. We should do well, therefore, to make Jesus our saviour and study to know the mind of God (Luke 9:35). No sorcery can overcome those who steadfastly remain committed to him (Numbers 23:23, Proverbs 26:2, 1 Peter 3:13-16).

Pavlov and awesome sorcery

Psychological and physiological experiments on dogs done by Ivan P. Pavlov, in his laboratory in Russia when the science of psychology was burgeoning in the first decades of the twentieth century, remain very relevant for the study of mental breakdown. Although these experiments may seem cruel by modern standards, they alerted the medical and psychological professions after the First World War to the similarity between the behaviour of dogs exposed to intolerable stress and the behaviour of soldiers

---

[15] Hitler's methods, after his miraculous demonic healing in 1918, are relevantly recorded by Lewis, D. (2003) *The Man Who Invented Hitler*. London, Headline.

exposed to intolerable stress in battle.[16] They showed that breakdown under excessive stress was natural and physiological, and therefore need not be classified as malingering.

Pavlov's experiments also showed how people could be manipulated involuntarily. More stress than can be coped with produces a state of nervous inhibition in the brain that acts as emergency protection by making the person insensitive to further gross assault but hyper-sensitive and hyper-reactive to small stimuli. So the person may seem paralysed in a sort of trance in the face of devastating trauma whilst minor stimuli produce exaggerated responses.

This is how a person may become hysterical, or even run amok. Eventually the person may physically collapse from exhaustion. It seems that the nervous inhibition includes the censor, the guard of the heart and mind. In this state the censor has been overwhelmed, so that the person's previous beliefs and old ways of making decisions may be abandoned, surprisingly readily, in favour of new ways that seem to offer the prospect of being saved out of the desperate situation. Thus the slate is wiped clean, as it were, and the person may then be manipulated.[17]

This sort of trance can be induced in healthy people after about thirty days' continuous fighting, bombardment and total disruption of life, or through similarly harrowing experiences. People are more likely to succumb if they are debilitated. They may also be inveigled into this sort of state by various forms of sorcery, such as the disclosure of awesome mysteries with music, drumming, dancing, weird lighting, incense, intoxicant drugs, the

---

[16] Pavlov's work only became available in English translation in 1941 and it had a major beneficial effect on the treatment of psychiatric battle casualties during the Second World War. See Pavlov, I. P. (1941) *Lectures on Conditioned Reflexes, Vol. 2, Conditioned Reflexes and Psychiatry,* translated with Introduction by Horsley Gantt, London: Lawrence & Wishart.

[17] A fairly detailed Christian account of all this, written before relativism and humanism became the fashion, may be found in Sargant, W. (1957) *Battle for the Mind*, London, Heinemann.

inducement of fear or panic, fasting, orgiastic indulgence, and other overwhelming, mind-blowing, shocking experiences that destroy preconception and belief. In this way a state of collapse may follow a wild night of dancing and drug taking in nightclubs or raves. And in this condition people may be suggestible and open to accepting all sorts of fascinating, tempting spiritual influences that can permanently change their lives. A similar state may follow a severe head injury. Severe shock and trauma can also induce a suggestible state, very suddenly, and demonic influences may gain an immediate hold.

Far less drastically, but just as effectively, if a person is trying very hard to concentrate with total dedication on something of vital importance, a similar state of trance may occasionally be produced if acute severe anxiety and sudden confusion should dramatically intervene.

Parts of the nervous system become inhibited and shut down under overloading stress. The parts of the nervous system that shut down are the parts that cannot handle the onslaught, sometimes because the onslaught unconsciously reminds the person of past experiences that have not been reconciled to God and healed.

Out of body experience

If the shutdown is extensive, the person may be semi-paralysed with shock and fear. The self-awareness and consciousness of the person may then actually feel separate from their body, so that the person may believe their soul or spirit to have left their body.

Such so-called out-of-body experiences may simply be deceptive. They can be explained by the overwhelming nature of the experience causing a protective inhibition and shutdown of areas of the nervous system concerned with proprioception, that is, of the sensory nerves that relay information about position and movement.[18] Spiritual beings can take advantage of this semi-paralysed and highly stressed state, however, and gain entrance to the soul to bring demonic life-changing revelation.

Personality change through Holy Spirit

In a person whose heart is absolutely committed to the God of Israel the Holy Spirit can also take advantage of this sort of condition. Paul had an experience like this, which is described in 2 Corinthians 12:2-4, in which he "was caught up into the third heaven. Whether it was in the body or out of the body I do not know – God knows."[19] Circumstantial events must have caused him to be unusually open to such a profound spiritual experience, although we are not told precisely what was going on for him then.

Most of us are usually so tied up with coping with the everyday concerns of this world that profound spiritual experiences like this are a rarity unless something really drastic happens.

Jacob, too, had a similarly powerful trance experience at the ford of the Jabbok, described in Genesis 32, in which he wrestled all night with a man who was God, although there is no suggestion that he actually felt out of his body. In fact God made sure Jacob's body remembered the event by injuring his hip joint. However, by the look of it, Jacob was extremely vulnerable at that time. He was trapped by people whom he had seriously offended. His life and the lives of all his immediate family were in danger. His uncle Laban threatened him from behind and his brother Esau from in front. Jacob, his wives and children, and all

---

[18] Ehrsson, H. H. (2007) *The Experimental Induction of Out of Body Experiences,* Science, Vol.317, No.5841, p.1048 and Lengennhager, B., Tadi, T., Metzinger, T., and Blanke, O. (2007) *Video Ergo Sum: Manipulating Bodily Self-Consciousness,* Science, Vol.317, No.5841, p.1096.

[19] This was not his Damascus road experience, which scholars tell us would have occurred more than fourteen years previously.

his possessions, could be lost whichever way he turned. Then his father's God, who had previously revealed himself to him in a dream, and in whom he ultimately placed his trust, wrestled with him till daybreak, and thereby changed his personality overnight. From then on, he was no longer a crafty dealer, but he was changed to become a patriarch honoured and blessed of God.

Daniel, too, was overwhelmed by a vision from God (Daniel 10). Moses, Isaiah, Jeremiah, Ezekiel, and many New Testament disciples are recorded as having intense spiritual experiences in which God communicated powerful messages to them.

In worship, if a person collapses under the influence of the Holy Spirit, the worship will usually have opened up the heart, mind and censor, so as to make the person suggestible, in a way that is safe, so that the Holy Spirit overwhelms that person.

Fasting can make a person more susceptible to this. Concentration will hopefully have been upon the person of the Lord Jesus in the message of the Spirit. It is kindest to allow a period of time to elapse for available areas of the soul to be affected by the Spirit, really spoken to, healed and changed. We do not know how long it took Paul to recover from having visited Paradise, but we know that when Paul first actually met Jesus on the road to Damascus (Acts 9) he was blind for three days and then went off into the desert for a good while (Galatians 1:17), and we know that Jacob wrestled with the man all night.

People who fall down under the influence of the Holy Spirit may need to lie there quietly for quite a while. Sometimes people may need a safe house for a week or two, or even for a year or two, like Paul had for three days at Straight Street. The preconceptions of the person's mind will be called into question, and this may take time. Fascinating, awe-inspiring possibilities may be presented to assume their place in the person's life, and to answer the deepest desires of the soul in a manner much more convincing and powerful than anything they have known before. The Holy Spirit may be working so deeply that we do not know what he is doing; but we should not impede the process.

Personality change through other spirits

If the process of spiritual change should be arrested or prevented, however, perhaps even by psychiatric treatment, a state of confusion and hopelessness could supervene. This may be suppressed with medication for the sake of putting on a good face. Or the process of spiritual change may be suppressed by agreeing to obey laws for the sake of social convention. But the moment of godly change and healing may be lost by being prevented in these ways. This could eventually precipitate chronic illness. Wisdom and spiritual discernment are needed.

It is not only the Holy Spirit that can overwhelm and change a person. Other powerful spirits can act in this way, too. The spiritual influence initiating the changes may not be of God. Indeed it may not even be the God of Abraham, Isaac and Jacob that the person is looking to. The Holy Spirit is not the only spirit to have power over people to change their lives like this. There are all sorts of spiritual powers that can prevail within people's souls once the defences are down.

Once the censor is put out of action as the attention of the person is gained, and the person is fascinated, entranced, captured, enraptured and enthralled, trance like states may be induced gently, seductively, gradually, almost imperceptibly, through all sorts of subtle forms of manipulation, domination, intimidation and control. They may also be induced violently through overwhelming domination that stuns the senses and rouses particular emotions. Or a combination of these means may be applied. And this may be done either knowingly, by people who know what they are doing, or unknowingly, by people who do not know what they are doing.

Family shackles

For instance, a person born into a family in which powerfully controlling forces operate may, from a tender age, be prevented from becoming the true person God made them to be. They may instead be expected and educated to be someone else, perhaps some other person they remind the family of or that the family thinks they should be, so that no opportunity becomes available truly to be creative with Holy Spirit and love and sound mind, or to develop freedom of will, or even to have their own mind or to be taken seriously. The person may be subtly constrained to develop into someone strangely necessary to the family or the local culture.

The false identity unwittingly imposed on a person may even be that of someone dead (in which case a spirit of death may be present), or of someone notorious, or of someone who failed to live up to expectations. The apparent hope may be that the family member will either emulate the other person and do better, or live out their curse and be like a scapegoat for the family. Such subtle domination may make a person feel imprisoned within a family without knowing why. The person will have been unwittingly entranced by a false identity that can become the cause of stresses and misunderstandings. They may eventually become torn apart with anxieties and confusions. This will particularly be the case if circumstances change to make it suddenly necessary to think independently and become self-reliant in a new way, as often happens in later adolescence when children move away from home. This sort of thing may become the cause of various mental illnesses, and it is fairly commonly found in anorexia nervosa and schizophrenia. It is worth noting that even Jesus had to cut himself free from his family (see Mark 3:31-35).

Healing comes after we ask the Lord to reveal bondages and wrong soul ties and false identifications in our lives, particularly with ancestors and our extended family. Then when we should forgive those responsible, confess the wrong relationships, renounce them, and ask God to break the bondages in the name of Jesus. Any associate demons should be expelled. We may then accept his healing. Then we find he will give us the courage to be more independent. In the course of time we shall discover he has put us on a firm foundation so that we can withstand strange and new circumstances, and still respect our family.[20]

Breakdown without the rock of salvation

If healing is not sought in the name of Jesus, new situations may be so daunting, however, that the stresses within the person from opposing ideas of equal hopelessness may seem like the stress of war. The person has been hitherto held in a sort of trance of false identity that is now proving inadequate. That person is not the person he or she has always been assumed to be, and the demands for autonomy made by a new culture may be daunting, because the true person has never been able to develop sufficient maturity to cope with change. In consequence, the person may feel they are disintegrating, and they may even become desperately frightened of death. Although the person may appear docile, in the absence of physical violence, that person may nevertheless feel on the verge of an abyss, impossibly torn between fight and flight, life and death, petrified of being engulfed by other people's solutions, terrified of being imploded by persecuting reality, all for no reason that anyone else may seem able to comprehend. When such a person gets cursed and rejected, wounded by accusation, madness of one sort or another may be expected to supervene.[21]

---

[20]For more detailed discussion I recommend Cross, D. (2007) *Soul Ties, the Unseen Bond in Relationships*, Lancaster, Sovereign World. Secular examples may be found in Laing, R.D. and Esterson, A. (1964) *Sanity, Madness and the Family*, London, Tavistock Publications.

[21] That schizophrenia may have this sort of explanation seems first to have been suggested by Gordon, W. (1948) in *Cerebral Physiology and Psychiatry*, Journal of Mental Science XC1V 118. There are interesting correlations with Bateson, G. (1973) *Steps to an Ecology of Mind*, St. Alban's, Paladin; with Laing, R.D. (1960) *The Divided Self*, London, Tavistock Publications; and with Kierkegaard, S. (1849) *The Sickness unto Death*. Some modern theories repudiate such studies; but they nevertheless seem corroborated by my experience and they seem particularly relevant for a Christian spiritual understanding.

Transference

Similarly, it is actually quite common to see other people who remind you of people from your past, and to behave towards them as though they actually were those people from the past. This phenomenon has been called 'transference', a word used by psychoanalysts.[22] A significant personality from the past is artificially but automatically transferred onto a person in the present. Your boss is seen like your dad for example. This sort of thing need not cause too much trouble if you are aware of the actual truth of the people involved in the present, and correct yourself. Healing may involve overcoming embarrassment and allowing oneself to become aware of the truth of what is going on. Then it will be necessary to bring past and present relationships before God for his healing.

However, if you continue to behave toward another person inappropriately, that person may feel caught by you in a sort of trance that they do not understand. If they are vulnerable, they may even collude with you, especially if you seem to meet some of their needs. Eventually, however, they may realise how powerfully and subtly they are being controlled by you. This is how paedophiles entice children, for example.[23]

Young children need to learn from an early age how to trust their misgivings about other people. Their opinions and reactions should be affirmed and discussed and taken seriously. They should learn to avoid being in any way seduced, and should be taught to ask the Lord, the Spirit of truth, to tell them who their friends should be and how to keep their integrity.

They should never be told to think differently in order to conform to polite expectations. They should not be made

---

[22] Early psychoanalysts should be given credit for alerting the modern world to this phenomenon.
[23] The paedophile will probably have been seduced in a similar way when he or she was a child. The paedophile's past needs healing.

biddable. They should not be forced into compliance. They need to be encouraged to defend themselves from a tender age.

Relationships that are fascinating but subtly unreal are best treated with great caution. This is the trouble, of course, with falling in love. Although there seems always to be an element of this in romance, it is probably best to be aware of it. It seems a good idea to learn to be able to catch yourself if you are seeing present acquaintances in the light of people from your past. Then, if past relationships are brought before the Lord for healing, it is possible to make the most of it if the right person comes along!

Transference may be used for healing

Transference is particularly likely to cause trouble if there are old, unresolved problems with certain people from your past. These are often sexual, although by no means exclusively so. By becoming aware of the inappropriateness of some of your feelings and behaviour towards certain people in the present, you may be able to find the Lord's healing for events that happened long ago that obviously continue to influence you.

To become aware of transference it is necessary for people to be very honest with each other and to meet in sincerity and truth (1 Corinthians 5:8) so that everything comes into the light, including all unclean spiritual influences and bondages, for the spell to be broken in order to be free. You must break wrong bondages and soul ties in the name of Jesus. In this way you will become much less vulnerable to being enticed and deceived through other people by Satan and his demons.

Deuced by suspense of judgement

Too much supposition, too much not really known, too much hidden seduction and manipulation, too many lies masquerading as truth, too much lying in the dark that cannot be truthfully spoken about, too much virtual reality, eventually make people confused. They become caught between opposing ideas that seem to have equal persuasiveness. So they simply live for the moment.

When it comes to making weighty decisions there is excessive debate. There is no firm foundation for thinking and believing, so the way they eventually act and react is determined by whimsy, compromise, and what feels good.

When we don't know who or what to believe we are at the mercy of who? or what? Who or what determines events? What power lies behind the show? Is there any absolute truth after all?

Most people seem to ride the crest of the wave of relativism and survive without ever thinking of the precariousness of their position. Quite a few of those people are in charge.

For others, something occurs to shake them. Some shock or adverse circumstance forces them to become aware of their insecurity. An accident, a war, a disaster, a death, an illness, a loss, an assault, a rejection, a fraught situation, makes them suddenly exposed and frightened.

Being caught between opposing ideas of equal power, when it seems important to make a judgement, can lead to a state of double-mindedness.

You can even become demonised by double-mindedness if, for example, you are caught between your better self and a false identity unwittingly insisted upon by other people. Perhaps you may have been looking to the people you live or work with in order to work out how to appear, but this is eventually causing conflicts within your soul. For some reason or other you feel unable to go along with them. The insecure person you truly are may not be sufficiently mature to handle the present situation decisively. So you either compromise, and bend over backwards to please and join the crowd, or you end up rejected, out of a job, perhaps even out of a home.

Compromise with the crowd can lead to loss of personal integrity, guilt and shame. Rejection can lead to bitterness, loneliness, self-pity. Either way, demonic forces can begin to torment you. For some people, sometimes, it can really seem as though there is nothing and no one definitely sound enough to prevent breakdown.

James recommends such double-minded people to "grieve, mourn and wail" and humble themselves before the Lord, then the Lord will lift them up (James 4:8-10). He will reveal truth, which is a firm foundation, and his still small voice will give direction.

Knowledge and wisdom hitherto accumulated through experience may suddenly prove insufficient when external circumstances change so as to threaten major elements of one's mind. Preconceptions and understanding now prove unsound. They seem to provide no firm ground for sound judgement. Other people may curse you for you indecisiveness and condemn you for your weakness. Whatever move you think to make seems to be wrong. You are unable to commit yourself to any decision or action. You are stultified, deuced[24] and trapped by opposing ideas. This can generate enormous internal stress within the soul and body, which effectively crushes the spirit, and threatens to cause dreadful breakdown through undermining the integrity of one's very being. It is only through God's sovereign, supernatural grace, accepting Jesus, receiving God's gift of repentance and (often) grieving, mourning, wailing, expelling demons in Jesus' name, holding on to God's promises in Jesus and proclaiming them true, and through faithful help from others, that a person may be lifted up and saved out of this sort of trouble and confusion when it has become extreme.

In 1 Timothy 6:20 and 21, Paul says, "Timothy, guard what has been entrusted to your care. Turn away from godless chatter and the opposing ideas of what is falsely called knowledge, which some have professed and in so doing have wandered from the faith. Grace be with you."

In this letter to Timothy, Paul was speaking of the disinterestedness of prevailing Greek culture. In the account of

---

[24] Deuced in the sense of pulled two ways, bedevilled, caught in conflict (see Partridge, E. (1958) *Origins* U.S.A., Macmillan). This old word has useful associations in this context.

Paul's visit to Athens, in Acts 17, the people there are described as spending their time "doing nothing but talking about and listening to the latest ideas", as many academics are in the habit of doing today. Greek scepticism denied the possibility of certain knowledge, and sceptics thus avoided firm belief, personal commitment and certain knowledge of God.

By setting equally strong propositions into opposition to each other,[25] a state of suspended judgement could be produced which left people alert but impassive, and open to new influences and possibilities to fascinate their intellects. Opposing ideas of equal relevance and power put the censor out of action. In effect they put the person into a kind of trance.

Scepticism, secularism and humanism

People are persuaded and subtly influenced these days, too, by similar means. Brilliant arguments are used to oppose and undermine weakly held systems of belief. These arguments are based more in theory than in knowing a truly faithful person or an almighty god. They bombard us with worldly facts and all sorts of make-believe and persuade us to suspend judgement. Then our minds and our values are changed for political and other reasons. Frequently this has been used as a device for manipulating change within a culture.

Meditation techniques and systems of physical stretching of the joints are popular means for inducing openness of soul and body so that personal change may be indiscriminately accepted. The subtle emphases of pictures and headlines in the media, and changes in the use of language, effected by pressure groups, reinforce required changes and prove spiritually far more compelling than they may seem at first to be. A state of semi-trance is induced in order that new ideas and beliefs, with their associated demons, may gain entrance to our minds and souls.

---

[25] Called by philosophers 'equipollence'.

This can usually be done without challenge because most people, particularly Christians, have all sorts of issues concerning spirit, soul and body that they have never taken to God for healing.

The power of old unhealed scenarios

Any major experience that cannot be made sense of may cause emotion or shock that threatens personal security by overwhelming the understanding and leaving the person unable to cope. Nevertheless, memory of the overwhelming experience will remain within the soul. Thereafter it will affect the censor, making it particularly sensitive to that pattern of unhealed events.

The person may be unable to face the full truth of what happened and may complain, "Why did this dreadful thing happen to me?" Then, although the censor has become particularly sensitive to the pattern of that unhealed experience, and shuns the full revelation of the truth of it, any potential opportunity to repeat the experience has a strange fascination. Clever arguments hook[26] in to material that seems relevant to unhealed issues, wherever it appears, so that people become fascinated by the unholy potential. In spite of one's self, repeating the scenario seems to have the potential for the safe and meaningful discharge of withheld emotion, which has been a hidden cause of stress.

If there should be another person present with sufficient godly love and wisdom to make it possible to come into the name of Jesus with the memory (as in Matthew 18:20), healing could actually begin to happen. Otherwise that particular pattern of unhealed experience will remain in the memory unhealed, and things and events that seem to be connected will have an uncanny fascination. Facts, information, imagination or

---

[26] The word 'hook' is used in this way in O'Brien, B. (1958) *Operators and Things*, New York, Arlington Books Inc., which is an account of schizophrenia.

experience that seems related to the unhealed memory may attract the person. This will unwittingly cause the person to be liable to manipulation, because the focus of attention would readily hook into all sorts of tempting potential solutions that may present themselves if it were not checked by the conscience. Other people whose scruples are not Christian may see this weakness and use it to control or exploit a person, and subtly lead them up the garden path towards destruction. The influence of past events can only be truly healed through Jesus.

For example, a small and rather childish youth, who had been exposed to sordid details of his mother's adventures as a prostitute, and neglected by her, was one day brutally and deeply wounded when girls he was out swimming with turned on him, stripped him of all his clothes and taunted him mercilessly about his masculinity. Thereafter he began to fantasise about vengeance. He began to be morbidly fascinated by beautiful women, increasingly obsessed with pornography, and determined to prove he was not inadequate. But women seemed increasingly reluctant to have anything to do with him. He turned to prostitutes but the absence of real relationship made him even more lonely and bitter. He stalked women who fascinated him. One night he raped a young girl. Subsequently, he was caught and sent to prison for a long time. The painful neglect and many wounds of childhood had never been brought to light to be healed. His fantasies and emotions about retaliating and being loved had obsessed him, and this weakness had been used by forces of evil in ungodly people to lead him into serious criminality and the destruction of his life.

The healing of early wounds of alienation, neglect and rejection, which are wounds to one's identity, making one deeply vulnerable in certain respects, can only be healed supernaturally through accepting Jesus. Without him they can seem overwhelming, so that the truth must be hidden behind the pain and confusion of a dysfunctional life. Until Jesus' healing is received, those wounds can be the root cause of fascinations, fantasies, obsessions and addictions that can ultimately destroy a person's life. With Jesus, however, all the facts can be faced, people can be forgiven and the power of obsessive behaviour can be broken. If a person would ask God for discernment in the name of Jesus Christ, and use what God reveals, and bring relevant issues before God into his light, accepting what Jesus did on the cross with repentance, so as to "take every thought captive for Christ" and find healing (2 Corinthians 10:5), not only would they no longer be manipulated but they would also find joyful freedom. But mostly people ignore God and do not do this. Therefore they continue to be manipulated and controlled like sheep by the prince of this world (Isaiah 53:6).

Television fascinates through giving vicarious expression to the thoughts, feelings and emotions of millions of wounded people. And it gives the illusion thereby that all will be well, since what you feel is what others feel, so your passions are not abnormal. In this way television reinforces cultural prejudices and gives people an excuse for not bringing their memories and activities into the light before the Lord for his healing. The same sort of mesmerising effect may be produced by emotive pictures, magazine stories, newspaper comment, rhythm and music, and also by the poetic idea that all mankind may be united in brotherhood by a magic goddess who so enraptures us that distinctive national, family and religious customs may be discarded and all be as one (as in Schiller's "Ode to Joy" sung in Beethoven's ninth symphony as the anthem of Europe).

Each individual is susceptible to all sorts of temptations to escape from difficulty and stress. Thus we are susceptible to being unwittingly led astray through being enraptured, and then manipulated. The fascinations of the world are everywhere. Unless we hold ourselves accountable to God in every aspect of our lives (Hebrews 4:13), even when we are tired or at a loss to know what to do, and unless we constantly maintain a real relationship with him through the Holy Spirit living in us, we are vulnerable. But if we follow the way God opens for us and continue to seek to be obedient and use the authority he gives us over the world, the flesh and the devil, in the face of opposition and difficulty, illness, trouble and suffering, he will increase our faith and courage and equip and perfect us. This involves ongoing repentance, discernment and godly wisdom. And we find his healing and joy, and remain free (2 Corinthians 3:17).

John tells us to test the spirits (1 John 4:1). So in order to guard our hearts (Proverbs 4:23) it behoves us to test the spiritual essence of everything that is, and has been, presented to us from our environment, especially of everything that seems to interest or fascinate us. It behoves us even to test what is presented in a credible way by our family or friends, by people we respect, by apparently authoritative people in the media, and in the name of Jesus in church. False prophets abound (Matthew 24:24). Every Christian needs the spiritual gift of discernment, with the self-control (1 Peter 5:8) which develops as a fruit of the Holy Spirit's work of healing (Galatians 5:22).

Rapture

Tremendous unbelief has developed since the two World Wars. People ask how God could have allowed such terrible things to happen. Surely, however, we are under God's judgement. Yet if Christians repent and turn away from deception and wickedness and persist in seeking God's face we may not only find his healing (2 Chronicles 7:14) but also find fellowship with others God is bringing to the wedding feast.

In extreme circumstances, such as battle or accident, in which we may find ourselves overwhelmed and perhaps even in some sort of trance-like state, God will save us, even enrapture us, even catch us up whether in the body or out of the body, if we know him and call on him in the name of the Lord Jesus Christ of Nazareth (Psalm 142:3a; Joel 2:32; 1 Thessalonians 4:17). This even includes moments when it may seem that we could go dangerously mad.

4

STRESS

Building character

We always move against resistance, even if hindered only by the atmosphere and the clothes we wear. Any movement from a state of rest is consequently accompanied by some degree of stress. Toil and sweat are inevitably to be expected in this fallen world. And stress comes not only from the endeavour to prevail against physical forces but also from the battle against intransigent human nature and other spiritual forces that may oppose us. Indeed the very existence of each one of us is the cause of some disturbance and stress for others.

If we lived at one with God, who created us in his own image (Genesis 1:27), we should have the complete rest he promises (Hebrews 4) but in this world there is always some degree of opposition, reluctance, or misunderstanding about what we do, what we feel and what we think (Genesis 3:17-19). Therefore even when we enter the Sabbath-rest God gives us in this world our rest is only relative.

When we have an everyday living relationship with God, the opposition we meet in this world produces perseverance, character, hope, and equipping for eternal life (Romans 5:3-4). For those who stay in the Lord, the stresses of everyday life, even though they may be extreme, build godly character so that godly wisdom accompanies knowledge (note Acts 7 and Acts 16:16-40). The activity of Holy Spirit in our souls and bodies uses the stresses of this world to build strength into the personality, much as exposure to winds strengthens the trunk of an oak.

It is not imperative, of course, that a person should have a relationship with God in order to develop character through prevailing against the world's adversities. But if there is no recognition of God, the Creator of the universe, the character will not be founded in relationship with God the rock (Matthew 7:24-27). Apparent strengths will be ungodly strongholds that the Lord will one day shatter. Godless people like this are everywhere, often in positions of authority.

Opposition in the workplace can sometimes be terrible. Many Christians return home exhausted from misunderstanding, false accusation, mockery, and manipulation. Those who simply brush off the day's work and determine to forget about it are avoiding a God-sent opportunity to grow and mature spiritually by yielding their experience to him and receiving his healing so as to become resilient to the sort of stresses he has been setting before them. Just to forget all the bother buries the experience and stores up trouble for later. We are to "work out our salvation with fear and trembling" (Philippians 2:12), "give thanks in all circumstances" (1 Thessalonians 5:18) and "consider it pure joy" when we face trials (James 1:2).

In order to remain healthy it is usually best to deal with the trouble as immediately as possible, to forgive and bless and be forgiven, to seek the Lord for clarification of issues, and for revelation and guidance, and so on. So after arriving home it may sometimes be necessary to spend a good long time resting in the presence of the Lord, receiving his healing and hearing from him, before doing anything else.

Human failing

When God is present it becomes apparent that each one of us is less than perfect in our dealings with the world. Sin is revealed. Not only do we sometimes mistake the word of God but also we quite frequently move away from God's presence. Each one of us fails so some extent to live according to our creator's instructions. Consequently our characters are less robust than they could be. Even those who live very close to God have trouble and sorrow and eventually lose their strength and die (Psalm 90:10). For the rest of us, the stresses and strains of everyday life may take a greater toll.

Jesus warned us about the uncleanness that may come out of our hearts, the evil thoughts, sexual immorality, theft, murder, adultery, greed, malice, deceit, lewdness, envy, slander, arrogance and folly (Mark 7:20-23). And he preached repentance before God and entry into the kingdom of God for cleansing. Amongst the consequences of his death on a cross and resurrection from the dead on the third day is that, by God's grace and through believing in him, we might be given kingdom power to overcome the iniquity and uncleanness that bring death. So Paul warned us to examine ourselves, to forgive others and to deal with our sin by confession and renunciation of it, and to accept of personal redemption through Jesus' blood and his victory on the cross, before breaking bread and drinking wine in remembrance of Jesus' death and resurrection. Otherwise we would be celebrating the new covenant in an unworthy manner and could, in consequence, become sick and die.

Sickness and sin

Whenever we do things, feel things, even think things that are not in accord with the Spirit of our creator, stresses occur within the soul and body that could weaken us so that we become more susceptible to evil, torment, illness and accident. We are made in the image of God and only find peace in our souls and bodies when we are right with him. Human nature has fallen away from his grace. Sin can come out of our hearts at any time if we let it, and inadvertently we often do so.

Furthermore, sickness can be caused through wrong relationships (Deuteronomy 7, Proverbs 1 to 8). Subtle wounds of the body and soul may cause sickness. And demons may cause sickness (Mark 9:14-32). And the sins of the ancestors inherited through the generations may cause sickness. My grandfather was a frustrated man who smoked tobacco, and so was my father, and so was I at one time, and far worse things than that can be handed down! All such things put us out of kilter with how God made us to be. They cause stresses in the living body, and in the mind, which beget sickness.

This is not theory. If you have eyes to see these things you find them all over the place. And it is astonishing that so many highly intelligent people who do not really know the Lord fail to connect the way they live with what they suffer.[27]

Habitual patterns of reaction to the multitude of environmental stresses and strains that make up our experiences are built naturally into our living physiology. And we cope automatically every day in the ways to which we have become accustomed. Our habitual ways of doing things will have established particular patterns of co-ordination of body functions that are mediated by the brain. Yet the Holy Spirit of God really can change all that and bring freedom, peace and permanent healing so that the work of God may be displayed in our lives.

Healing in the presence of God

Jesus implied in John Chapter 9 that it was neither that the blind man had sinned nor that his parents had sinned that really mattered. The fact is that we are all sinners (1 John 1:10). That can be taken for granted. What mattered was that the work of God should be displayed in our lives. Neither the King James version of John 9 in the Bible, nor the New International Version, make this clear, although other versions do so (Moffatt, Good News Bible, New English Bible).

In fact for those with eyes to see it there is a clear connection between sin and illness throughout the Holy Bible - see Mark 2:1-12, Romans 6:23, James 5:16 and, not least, Deuteronomy 28.[28] And healing is available in the kingdom of heaven and amongst those who walk with the Lord.

---

[27] As demonstrated in most of the books in the bibliography.

[28] This subject is more extensively dealt with in my book *Healing for the Wounded Life*.

Our God is the God of peace and his only begotten Son is the Prince of peace and all authority in heaven and on earth has been given to him (Isaiah 9:6, Matthew 28:18, 1 Corinthians 14:33, etc.). This means he desires to bring his supernatural peace into the spirit, soul and body (Romans 8:11) of each one of us, peace that the world cannot give, so that our hearts should not be troubled (John 14:27), peace that can be felt in our bodies through sense perception. When we feel this peace we know his presence.

The classical Greek word 'doxa', which is translated as 'glory' in the New Testament (in this context notably in 2 Corinthians 3:16-18) implies sense perception of real presence. It implies the appearance of God.[29] The presence of God in our lives not only brings freedom, as our stresses are removed and we really receive God's healing so as to reflect his glory, but if his Spirit lives in us we shall also bear fruit for his glory through our relationships (1 Corinthians 10:31).

Therefore Solomon says God's word brings health to the whole body. This proves to be true. So we should do well to feed on the word of God in scripture. Solomon also recommends that we guard our hearts, for our hearts are the wellspring of life (Proverbs 4:20-23). The heart of the soul is the seat of desire and will. Therefore we should do well to take care about whom we open our hearts to. And since our minds play an important part in guarding our hearts we should take care, too, about what we allow into our minds.

God's word heals

Solomon's words also indicate that we could die from lack of discipline, and he says that if we keep God's commands we shall live (Proverbs 5:23 and 7:2). Holy Spirit, who comes to us after we accept what Jesus did for us on the cross, brings us into loving relationship with God, and gives us understanding so that we see

---

[29] From Derek Prince's (1972) teaching on Bible Psychology.

things God's way, which makes the discipline Solomon speaks about something actually to be desired. When we read scripture with Holy Spirit, God's commands become loving guidance for everlasting life.

And clearly, if we take scripture seriously, healing will be found in the company of those who come together into the name, that is into the presence, of the Lord Jesus (Matthew 18:20). He healed then, and surely he will heal now (Matthew 28:18-20).

Cultural unbelief hinders healing

The trouble is that too many cultural strongholds in our minds too often block out his presence. We are sceptical and we doubt, we prefer the certainty of science and technology to faith in any person, our minds are unwittingly full of advice from the media, stuck in humanistic philosophical concepts and biased by legalistic religion.

Furthermore, scientific medicine is forbidden by law from bringing spiritual matters into play. And many Christian leaders prefer to leave in the hands of secular specialists the sometimes tortuous process of bringing God's healing into the lives of sick people in this scientific age.

Although this is not a medical textbook, it is necessary in the following chapters to take a critical look at some medical diagnoses, and at a little medical science, and to discover how the Holy Spirit may break through to heal. General description of conditions, using some common medical terms, is accompanied by aids to understanding how it is possible with the Lord to avoid becoming ensnared by them. And sometimes we can learn significant lessons from rather more extreme considerations.

Drugs

The drugs developed by pharmaceutical companies to treat stress, and related emotional, psychological and physical conditions, mostly affect the physiology of the brain and nervous system. These drugs are what most people, and their doctors, trust to alleviate such problems and keep going. The cortex of the brain is a complex interconnecting and co-ordinating network through which sensory information is received and behavioural responses initiated. Personal behaviour involves constant subtle interrelating physiological changes, within the brain and the whole of the living body, in relation with the people and events in the environment. Patterns of arousal are established through the reticular activating system. Patterns of emotion are established through the limbic system. And the concomitant endocrine and autonomic adaptations, involving regulation of body temperature, appetite, thirst, metabolism, the cardiovascular system, reproductive system, water and electrolyte balance and excretion of urine are regulated through the hypothalamus in the brain.

Various chemical neurotransmitters are involved at synapses, where a nerve fibre joins another nerve. These neurotransmitters include dopamine, noradrenaline, serotonin, acetylcholine, histamine, endorphins and prostaglandins. Various drugs, such as antidepressants and antipsychotics, can be used to increase or decrease the release or reuptake of these neurotransmitters and thereby to control mood and behaviour, and thus to control distress.

Mental and physical depletion

So-called mental illness arises when established pathways by which a person has hitherto coped become overwhelmed. Adequate alternatives cannot be found naturally, and so reserves are depleted. Particular environmental stresses to which the person has become sensitive may trigger devastatingly vicious circles of thought, emotion and behaviour that break the person down both mentally and physically. Physical exhaustion generates mental stress and mental exhaustion generates physical stress in a vicious circle. Exhaustion and depletion of reserves may lead to burnout and, if this is complicated by chronic bitterness, torment, hopelessness, or resignation it is called depression. Compensatory coping mechanisms may be socially unacceptable and may consequently lead to the diagnosis of illness. The Prince of this world certainly knows how to bring this sort of thing about. Yet God's promise to us is that whoever calls on the name of the Lord will be saved (Joel 2:32; Proverbs 18:10).

At worst some people get so stressed that they can only regain their strength through rest and tolerant hospitality, with very generous personal attention, often including much regular and sincere talk over a considerable period of time. Meanwhile doctors may use sedation with various drugs that act on neurotransmitters, in order to force a person to calm down and rest for a while artificially. After all, not only may the body be exhausted but also the censor and the conscience may be so seared by devilish attacks as to be rendered powerless, and distort the mind. Confusion may be made worse through loss of energy. Discernment and will may lose their power. The person can become further traumatized and stressed through being too worn out and biddable, and may thus be led astray, and used and abused. This way the human spirit may be broken, and body and soul may live in great stress for many years, struggling to hold together.

Then even small disturbances can trigger excessive reactions, even violence or suicide. This tendency can even occasionally be exacerbated by some of the drugs prescribed by secular medical practice; so it is necessary for doctors to be careful. Nevertheless drug treatment is entirely reasonable in such situations. It should, be used with wisdom, however, and with the understanding that God's healing is available.

Healing through fellowship

It is often possible to engage with the person, and to allow the presence of God to begin to heal whilst treatment with medication continues. Occasionally, however, if medication obliterates sensitivity and prevents adequate recall, a person may need slowly to be taken off some or all of the drugs, and carefully nursed back to better health, before they can really begin to deal before God with the roots of their wretchedness.

So if mental and emotional breakdown have occurred, there may eventually be a lot of catching up to do. Shock and trauma may need the Lord's healing. Emotion that has been held on to, and has not been admitted to or understood, not brought into the light for God's healing, will have caused prolonged stresses. Feelings are meant to be felt, after all - they put us in touch with reality. Unless we admit to them reality is distorted. Emotions in themselves they are not evil. But repressed emotion with confusion can eventually lead to excessively expressed emotion at some relaxed moment when there is a reminder. Unless this is met with healing, the person may be re-traumatized. To make matters worse, demons may have attached themselves to unhealed emotions, and they can cause considerable havoc. If this is the case, they can be authoritatively bound up by those who know the Lord Jesus until all the shock and trauma is healed in the presence of God (See 1 Peter 2:21-25).

The events and memories and thoughts associated with all those unhealed and debilitating emotions should ideally have been submitted to God immediately, laid on the cross for Jesus to carry, and thus reconciled with God moment by moment, so that he will heal and give direction. When you have been walking with the Lord through all sorts of troubles for a good long time, this sort of process can become fairly automatic. But there are times when this simply seems impossible, even for mature Christians. This world is full of violence. We must be prepared to help each other. And when all seems lost the Lord is still present to save (Psalm 31:21-22 and Psalm 34:17-18).

Dealing with emotions

The beginning of the healing process, when the time and place become available, may go something like this: "I hate you. I could kill you for what you have done. However, because I accept that Jesus died for my own sins and rose from the dead the third day and I know myself to be forgiven for having done the same sort of things that you have done, I release you into my forgiveness and bless you. God bless you! Father, please forgive me for my murderous hatred and heal me in Jesus' name. I receive your forgiveness and healing, Father. Thank you for sending your only begotten son Jesus to redeem us."

Sometimes the emotions need to be very openly expressed, and then given to the Lord so that he may salt them with his fire as we thank God for Jesus. Then the soul may be tempered, as excesses are burned up by God, and self-control develops. In even more extreme cases a person may need to live separated from the world for a while, in the presence of the Lord with the Lord's people, in a safe house where everyone assists with each other's everyday tasks. Sometimes it can take a long time, with a lot of straight talking, for sufficient trust to develop for lives to be sorted out.

We live in a fallen world full of fallen stress. Not being yourself and acting a part is stress. Putting on a face is stress. Always reacting to other people's demands without listening to God is stress. Excitement is stress. Emotions and thoughts not reconciled to God are stress. Not having God's peace and truth, and not allowing yourself to have time with him, is stress. Our human nature is sinful. Our own strength is insufficient for us to live God's way. It is necessary to acknowledge the truth of this before God. We may overcome, and live in his kingdom of peace with a foretaste of what is to come (2 Corinthians 1:22), only through Jesus, who was raised from the dead. Through the Holy Spirit he brings resurrection power to those who know and love him.

If expressed emotion has actually wounded other people, it can be sorted out, with God's help, by forgiving and being forgiven and by accepting that another person is entitled to their personal experience and emotions and thoughts and opinions, and by receiving God's healing in spirit, soul and body for mistakes that have been made. This way people get free of each other, and are no longer encumbered with unnecessary guilt, involvements, memories, and influences. Some people call this sort of thing "breaking soul ties".

Serious stress

When feelings are not dealt with like this, sin gets hold of the heart because natural responses have not been released through confession (see Proverbs 28:13, James 5:16, 1 John 1:9). Then demons may get a foothold, and will have to be expelled in the name of Jesus in order to be rid of them. A heart operating with guilt, fear, shame, frustration, worry, anger, unforgiveness, hatred, apprehension, shock, fatigue, envy, lust, or any of all the other natural emotions stuck within it, stresses not only itself but also the whole soul and body. Wearing the heart on the sleeve, as they say, helps accountability; but what really counts is admitting emotions to God through Jesus, and walking humbly before him.

Increases in the secretion of cortisol and adrenalin occur when emotions are held in the dark. These are hormones that adjust the physiology to cope with stress. Their concentration in the blood can be measured in a laboratory. Such long-term stresses cause illness, both mental and physical.[30]

Stress weakens the body, depletes reserves of energy, confounds and confuses thought and behaviour, seriously hinders healing, and undermines self-control so that emotional responses may become excessive and wound the person further. Deficiencies appear in coping ability. Personal disintegration threatens. In extreme cases ordure and urine may be excreted inappropriately, and the ability to be embarrassed may be lost. As the person falls apart it may even cease to matter to them who catches them or what they use to try to stay intact.

---

[30] See the latest edition of Henry W. Wright *A More Excellent Way – Be In Health* published by Pleasant Valley Church, Thomaston, Georgia, 30286, USA. See www.beinhealth.com. He and his co-workers have demonstrated how the biochemistry of stress debilitates physiologically, and they have painstakingly discovered spiritual mistakes that commonly lead to specific illnesses.

In other people chronic stresses cause physical illness. Every sort of illness may be related to unresolved issues. It is always worth asking the Lord to reveal them.

Therefore do not give store-room in your heart to natural responses that have not been yielded to God. Get the Holy Spirit sealed in your heart so that he can check everything!

What is under the surface is grist to the mill

Of course, most people do not have much true notion of what is deep in their hearts, at the back of their minds, or in their genes. Everything unnecessary for the immediate present is banished out of mind. Why bring up things that are unpleasant?

Well, you can live like this until you are brought up sharply. You can assume that being stressed all the time is part of your nature until something happens that shatters you. But then you will not know why you should feel so wretched or be so ill!

Sometimes it is necessary to find a safe time and place where issues that need to be revealed may be brought to God for healing in the name of Jesus. This is not self-indulgence, it is self-protection.

Although all that has been hidden in the dark may seem to represent an apparently confused, unlovable side of yourself, it is wise to make regular time for fellowship with genuine people so that through godly relationships the Holy Spirit may probe the dark recesses of your soul and reveal hitherto hidden aspects. Talking personally, and overcoming the embarrassment so commonly associated with frankness, is a good idea. It may be most appropriate, amongst people who take God seriously, particularly to use the Sabbath for mending meetings.

What can you do if you keep falling into panic or despondency? You cannot afford to hold on to your respectability. God complains, "They do not cry out to me from their hearts but wail upon their beds." (Hosea 7:14.) You need not keep on avoiding being embarrassed! The Holy Spirit knows everything anyway (1 Corinthians 2:10-11) and he knows that what you wail about on your bed stresses you out. He wants you to know his healing and his peace. God works through his people with love.

Relevant feelings and thoughts and memories may more readily appear as you join with other people and come together into the name of Jesus and seek his face and his words together. Then the truth of what is going on in a person's life may be revealed, particularly when the Lord Jesus is worshipped and as Scripture is read. What comes up should all be given to God. Issues from the dark, and from the hitherto forgotten past, no matter how unspeakable they have been, may then begin to be healed.

It is a fact that if even a desperate, mentally ill person is met personally and truthfully in the Holy Spirit like this, healing begins because Jesus is present. Although drugs may be necessary for a time, the true body of Christ is much better than drugs, and the Holy Spirit can break through the strongholds of the mind and bring the peace the world does not understand right into the spirit operating the central nervous system.

"There remains, then, a Sabbath-rest for the people of God..." (Hebrews 4:9).

5

ANXIETY, ADDICTION, PHOBIA, OBSESSION

Nature and causes of anxiety

The emotion naturally felt when your position seems undermined, when there is uncertainty about a significant outcome, when you feel inadequate to face a situation, and when you do not know where to turn, is, of course, anxiety.

It can be felt in relation to a disconnection, a misjudgement, or a misunderstanding with other people that threatens your security. The fault may or may not be yours, but you may not be able to determine where you stand.

Or perhaps you are on some sort of new threshold, entering unknown territory, thinking you'll not cope and dreading an inability to find peace and self-control. It is quite common to be caught between an abyss of apprehension and meaninglessness on the one hand and having to put on a good face and act in an acceptable way on the other.

In extreme situations anxiety may be described as anguish, or as being in dire straits. [31]

Anxiety is perceived in the body as nervousness, apprehension, stress, and hypersensitivity and, in more drastic situations, as panic, unreality, and dread. Physical symptoms may become observable, such as sweating, muscular tension, light-headedness, trembling, palpitations, shortness of breath, epigastric discomfort, nausea, looseness of the bowels. When it is prolonged it leads to physical exhaustion, as described above.

---

[31] Søren Kierkegaard (1844) *The Concept of Anxiety* and Sigmund Freud (1926) *Inhibitions, Symptoms and Anxiety* are worth reading on this subject. But the Holy Bible is best: note Deuteronomy 28:65.

These are very natural reactions to difficult situations. The causes, however, may sometimes be far from clear. The Holy Spirit knows what is going on, nevertheless. If he lives in you, he will reveal all you need to know if you open your heart to the Lord.

You may well benefit from the help of other people with this. Eventually the Lord will lead you to safety and peace, provided you allow him to do so by placing your faith in him, rather than in your feelings or in anything, or any one, else.

Fundamental ontological insecurity

A sort of chronic anxiety, accompanied by boredom, ennui and dread, arises out of a state of fundamental insecurity in your very existence when you have no godly vision. No revelation appears that is ultimately adequate, or good enough, for the desires of the heart, which have naturally been generated by perceived circumstances. Proverbs 29:18 speaks of this state of mind: "Where there is no vision, the people perish" (KJV). Ecclesiastes 1:2 and 12:8 speak of it as vanity or meaninglessness: "Everything is meaningless". It comes from a failure to acknowledge the presence of God, and from failing to perceive what he is doing and to make one's peace with him.

The feelings of abandonment, exposure and vulnerability associated with such ontological insecurity commonly result in people using their deductive reasoning to find human solutions to their various predicaments. It also results in people doing whatever they want. The inventiveness of the human mind can be very exciting. Possibilities for entertainment seem endless. Scientific discoveries seem wonderful. Logical reasoning seems a sound basis for policy and action. But when God is excluded and his direction unheeded, there is ultimate dissatisfaction, frustration, and eventually disaster. People commonly deny this, of course; but the pursuit of healing will not allow us this luxury.

The ontological insecurity and hidden chronic anxiety of humanist culture was known over five thousand years ago. It is described in Genesis 3, particularly in verses 7 and 10. The story is told there of Adam and Eve losing God by being tempted away from him through the rebellious suggestions and camouflaged pride of the serpent, who was Satan. Their eyes were opened as they accepted his fruit, but their spirit died. They became able to reason about good and evil. Conscious awareness of the fallen world developed through their anxiety, as they discovered their nakedness and vulnerability.

The fallen state of mankind continues. Fear, worry, apprehension, guilt, shame and frustration commonly accompany anxiety, whether it is acute or chronic. All these emotions, and others, may powerfully accompany anxiety according to the situation. They are particularly found when education has been lacking, intellectual concepts have not been developed and no opportunity seems to be available to achieve the worldly success that is secretly envied.

Of course anxiety is a natural reaction, natural to the fallen state of humanity which we all share. It only becomes classified as illness when a person consults a doctor who considers it to be excessive, which need not always be the case. Doctors may add the term 'neurosis' to make it sound more like an illness, which may make the condition seem to be more serious than it really is. The term 'neurosis' simply means 'a condition of the nerves'.

It is important to be aware, of course, that the actual causes of anxiety in this fallen world, whether it be classified as an illness or not, may lie either inside yourself or outside yourself – and commonly both. Your anxiety may be due to some personal weakness or other – perhaps due to events of your life that have not been healed - or it may be due to environmental threats that may or may not be obvious, or both. And of course confusion may make anxiety much worse.

It is also important to be aware that the presence of the Lord Jesus, the presence of his Spirit, will remove insecurity, heal anxiety, and bring us back as it were into oneness with God in the

Garden of Eden. We may cast all our cares on him (Psalm 55:22 and 1 Peter 5:7).

Social dynamics of anxiety

Other people's behaviour, emotion and stress may generate anxiety in you until you can determine the cause of it - particularly until you know whether or not you are the cause of it. In that case it could be sorted out by opening up discussion, bringing relevant issues to light, and seeking godly reconciliation. Of course, this could take time. And in the short term it may prove impossible because of resistance due to various prejudices from unhealed past experiences, as previously described.

In this fallen world it is usually necessary for people to express emotion in order to know where they stand with each other. Provided there is no violence, truth may be openly recognised this way, and facts established. If the emotions of everyday life are openly expressed, yielded to God and put right with him, the accompanying anxieties and stresses may be transient. But if emotions are not admitted to, openly confessed and brought into the light, there can be confusion and deception, and other people will be made anxious because of all the uncertainty.

The effort of controlling yourself (whether consciously or automatically) so as not to reveal emotion may cause anxiety and stress both in yourself and in other people. People who are stressed make other people anxious. They are subliminally aware that anxiety is in the air, particularly if the reason is unclear. This induces reserve and fear so that misunderstandings develop. This way, relationships can become unreal. And this sort of situation can become chronic so that chronic stresses of mind and body and behaviour develop from chronic anxieties in families, institutions and communities. Furthermore, people may become so used to this sort of apparently intractable situation that they hardly notice the fact of it. It takes supernatural godly discernment to discover the truth of what is going on.

The expression or manifestation of anxiety, or any other emotion for that matter, in a potentially hostile environment, amongst people who are unwilling to bring relevant issues truthfully to light, will indicate to them that you may be vulnerable. If they perceive any lack of self-control they will naturally reckon that your emotion could perhaps be exploited. They could even decide to use it against you for their own advantage. In such a situation you will probably sense something in the air and automatically be suspicious, and on the defensive. To some extent you will prepare for fight or flight, in case anything should go wrong. So the stress hormones of your body will become active.

It is common to try to disguise such vulnerability either with aggression or with watchful reserve, either in the belief that attack is the best form of defence or in the belief that you could be overwhelmed at any moment. So you may seem hypersensitive. People may even accuse you of paranoia, whilst denying they have played any part in your state of mind.

Only by maintaining a constant relationship with the Holy Spirit will you keep your peace in such a situation. Holy Spirit will keep you sincere and truthful about your emotions and thoughts and about your perception of what has been going on. He will show you what to say and give you firm ground to stand on amongst people who are hostile (2 Timothy 4:16-18). Certainly, however, it may help to have some confirmation of your position by talking it through at a suitable moment, with an intelligent, humble and unbiased person who has the Spirit of truth in them.

It is particularly significant that after a Christian comes into Holy Spirit baptism, and really knows the peace of God in the heart, it becomes apparent that anxiety is the result of moving away from a close living relationship with God into unrighteous enemy territory.[32] So anxiety and lack of peace can be valuable warning signs of unrighteousness and impending trouble.

Security through validation of perception

In order to try to understand more about the basic nature of anxiety, in a way that seems to correspond with the Bible, we should go back to the beginning, to just after a baby has been born (as David did in Psalm 139 - note verse 23). When mother and baby first look into each other's eyes, their mutual recognition is a continuation of the intuitive relationship that had preoccupied the mother when the child was in the womb.[33] From that moment on, if there is good-enough security in that relationship, the child knows it is possible to meet the mother with sufficient truth and love to go on to make sense of the world. Thereafter, children need to be met by parents in respect of every significant aspect of their experience in order to avoid excessive anxiety and discover meaning, and truth about salvation, and in order to develop a sound-enough basis of godly sense about everyday matters to grow into independent adults. Parents who avoid legalism and have a lively relationship with the Holy Spirit will thus build sound foundations into the characters of their children.

Without the experience of overcoming significant obstacles that cause anxiety in all sorts of situations, so as to know how the peace of God may be found with healing and reconciliation and righteousness, the development of meaning and intelligence will lack sound foundation. To some extent God's peace will fail to

---

[32] Cross D. (2008) *God's Covering - a Place of Healing*, Lancaster, Sovereign World.
[33] Winnicott, D.W. (1956) *Primary Maternal Preoccupation* in *Collected Papers* (1958), London, Tavistock Publications. When this preoccupation goes wrong for one reason or another, and this basic anxiety affects the relationship with the unborn child it seems possible that <u>autism</u> may result. God will begin to heal this condition, however, after the autistic person seeks his face for healing and comes into the presence of the kingdom of God. Pregnant mothers would do well to keep speaking truth to their unborn babies and praying for them.

come to soul and body, so that the child will live with hidden stresses and inevitably suffer some excess of basic insecurity and anxiety (Psalm 85:10, Hosea 2:19-20) until healing is perhaps found later.

Mankind's difference from animals

In this respect mankind differs from the animals, who do not feel such anxiety. We can sense that animals feel emotions, such as fear and worry and frustration, but when they sense something is wrong they react according to their nature, and the instincts of the herd suffice. They do not know insecurity in their very being and the deep anxiety, alienation, dread, guilt, shame and sickness of mind and body that may come from not in any way glorifying God of their own free will (Romans 1:20-21), nor do they have the sense of peace and freedom that comes from righteousness. This difference is proof that mankind is made in the image of God. Later this will be seen to be of particular relevance to discussion about schizophrenia.

Healing

People who suffer from chronic anxiety and insecurity may seek God's guidance for their healing with great benefit. This is achieved through coming to Jesus. Although the causes may not at first be obvious, God will reveal what needs to be known at the appropriate moment, and he will heal through the power of the Holy Spirit if he is asked to do so in the name of Jesus, and if his words are heeded. Over a period of time the Holy Spirit may reveal aspects of one's past life, and of the sins of one's family and ancestors. Sometimes the emerging details may be distressing, of course. And frequently the Lord will use aspects of one's present relationships in order to try to draw one's attention to events and relationships from the past that need healing. Old habits die hard and they affect every aspect of the way one's life is conducted. Memories, misperceptions, habits and behaviour that should be put right with him are often repeated in present circumstances. So one's behaviour may not always be entirely appropriate. Through becoming aware of this, and subsequently allowing repentance and forgiveness and deliverance, and new ways of perceiving and thinking, God can bring profound relief and healing.

After an event (often a childhood event, but not necessarily so) that was in some sense too overwhelming to come to terms with, your imagination can develop fantasies that may become quite powerful. The fantasies may develop into compulsive behaviour, addictions or obsessions. Healing comes through bringing all related true facts to light and making peace with God.

Most frequently this sort of work on yourself may be best done in a group of Christians with whom you regularly meet. Sometimes it may be necessary to find a particular safe place amongst sincere and truthful people for as long as it may take to do some work on yourself like this with God. Occasionally, this work of sanctification and healing may best be done through regular meetings, over a period of time, with a particular minister, or elder, or a Christian psychotherapist or counsellor. Expressing yourself openly, without censorship, sometimes even using some creative activity like painting pictures or making music, can bring relevant material to the surface.

Addiction and lust

If you have tried to find solutions for your difficulties and problems in your own strength rather than with God's help, emotions such as anger, rejection, stubbornness, fear, insecurity, and frustration, may have become firmly attached to all the anxieties and the stress inside you. Those reactions naturally provide for your self-protection and self-justification. And they will automatically be triggered into action when anxiety and stress are uncomfortable.

Some relief may also have been found through blaming and rejecting those who have seemed to cause you difficulty, and by becoming irritable, and so on, rather than by seeking revelation and truth from God, and forgiving and being forgiven.

The stress of holding on to natural emotions, and failing to give them to God by laying them on the cross of Jesus, may naturally be assuaged by material comforts. Unredeemed human nature will use whatever seems immediately to hand to make things feel easier. Alcohol, tobacco, drugs, entertainments, and all sorts of other distractions are immediately available palliatives But they all have a sting in their tail.

The logic and the comforts of this world offer only temporary relief. Ultimately they fail to fulfil their promise. They are like sucking your thumb because your mother's breast is unavailable. They lead eventually to a sense of futility, although it may take many years for this to be realized. Meanwhile the substances get their hooks into you. Everything conspires to make you believe you cannot manage without them. Relying on them, can make you lust after them continually, and become utterly addicted to them. Your life is controlled by your compulsion to obtain the object of your addiction. Only when you reach the rock bottom of utter hopelessness do you find the sense to try to get free.

Human nature easily leads us to become caught in attachments to worldly objects like this, and in behaviours that eventually bring all sorts of poison and trouble of their own. The excitement of attaining the object of your lust, whether it be a substance or a gambling win, stimulates production of adrenalin, and the adrenalin rush itself becomes addictive. So does the relief of getting what you want.

When many wounds have been hidden and plenty of excitement and ready comforts are easily available, and a person has lost hope of finding any real healing peace, an eventual sense of emptiness and restless fatigue, ennui and discouragement may eventually crush the spirit. The body will have become exhausted through overindulgence. Resilience will be depleted. Serious physical illness may have set in. All the energy will have been wasted without any lasting satisfaction. Jaded cynicism and alienation, and many demons acquired along the way, will allow no real rest. And deadly worn-out rakes attract their own kind. And certainly we can learn from their experience.

Getting free involves meeting the Lord Jesus whose blood was shed to redeem you, and who died on the cross and rose from the dead. It involves coming into the kingdom of God through Jesus, coming in from the cold, receiving the new life he gives you. Demons of addiction cannot abide his presence. They must leave sooner rather than later. After that, it will be best to re-examine and readjust the whole of your life, which may take quite a long time. The help of other people who have got free from similar situations can be invaluable.

The process may be a battle; but the love of God will win through. With perseverance and endurance the enemy will be overcome by the Lord of lords. After all, who wants to be a slave? Freedom is available! Baptism in Holy Spirit and speaking in tongues is powerfully effective.[34]

Overactive children (ADD)

In this same sort of way so-called hyperkinetic disorders and attention deficit disorders, ADD (these are medical terms for over-activity and poor concentration) are produced in young people. The difference is that youngsters take longer than adults to become worn out, and their addiction is to frenzy.

One lad, who was most distressingly hyperactive, demanding constant attention and never able to concentrate, had an elder brother who was always playing tricks to land him in trouble, so that the lad would repeatedly be punished for what he had not done. This lad never knew who his father was. His mother claimed not to know which man had made her pregnant with him. She rejected the lad, and always believed what the elder brother told her. She would never offer forgiveness to the

---

[34] See Jackie Pullinger's book *Chasing the Dragon.*

younger child. I suspected that her youngest reminded her of her shame, and that she hated herself for her promiscuity. But in consequence, the lad was utterly insecure. There seemed no way for him to know the truth about anything. He was trapped in a merciless world without any apparent right or wrong, in which he constantly had to fight to survive. No wonder he was frenetic.

If all meanings are of equal value and choices depend on how a situation takes you, there is no ultimate truth, no ultimate peace, and nothing really matters. If you love, you are going to get hurt. If you do not love, you are going to get hurt. So it may seem logical to try to become good at being hurt. Pain is real; it has meaning. It can even be something to hold on to, something constant in a world of relativity. And it gives you natural energy to fight.

This is the humanistic, pagan world such children live in. They have never known the love and truth that can bring healing and peace. There is no sure foundation for anything, so anything goes. They get what they want however they may. And what they want is often addictive, assuaging the stress they live with.

It can be costly to try to bring truth and the love of Jesus to them. To persist in loving those who manipulate, deceive, rob and even hate you, and to persevere in speaking truth with love despite rejection, mockery, unbelief and all sorts of misgivings, can bring much heartache; but you have to survive for the sake of those young people. This can be valuable training for a Christian. One day they may see Jesus in you.

Panic and temper tantrums

Frenetic behaviour is closely related to <u>panic</u>, which may supervene when anxieties become desperate. The person urgently keeps trying to cope but no longer feels able to do so. Calling on God in the name of Jesus seems not to work.

Excuses for having become too desperate to heed his reply are quite common. Powerful emotions, however, may be surfacing in response to the challenges being faced. The controls seem to be failing as the situation becomes overwhelming. Confusion makes anxiety worse.

Over-breathing is common and may lead to faintness. A good remedy for this is to put a large paper bag or towel over the head so that the air breathed in is the air that was just breathed out, which will therefore contain more carbon dioxide and cause air hunger, which will often stop the over-breathing.

Panic with over-breathing like this is frequently found to be an attempt to control deeper emotions, such as anger or weeping. There may be a scream underneath. The person may even be about to run amok – and this can be dangerous, so it should be stopped by physical restraint using as much kindness as possible.

Temper tantrums in children are best treated in the same way – with loving restraint and kindly holding.

Physical symptoms may be frightening and add to the panic – such as feeling unreal with palpitations, dizziness, chest pain, or choking. And other fears, of dying or of going mad for example, may make matters even worse. Continuing to address the situation firmly but gently, with godly authority, truth, justice and compassion, and deliverance from a spirit of fear in the name of the Lord Jesus, will bring peace.

Fears and phobias

Fear can very easily become associated with things or with situations that provoke anxiety. And such fear is easily reinforced, so that the person gets programmed with the fear. Fear and panic may then appear automatically, simply when triggered by the thought of a particular situation.

The psychological medical word for this is phobia, which means an extreme or irrational fear or aversion. Agoraphobia, for example, is an habitual fear of open spaces that may be triggered in previously wounded individuals just by the thought of leaving home or of being in public places. Social phobia, describes the habitually fearful avoidance of social situations. Alternatively, fear may be triggered by flying in aircraft, by darkness, by spiders and mice and bats, and by all sorts of other potential situations that seem threatening. Such fears and phobias will be found to be associated with events that may have caused profound distress and panic in the past.

To find healing it is necessary to come into the real presence of God in the name of Jesus and be rid of the demon of fear by commanding it out in Jesus' name. It will then be possible to deal with what the anxiety and fear were really all about and reconcile the issues to God.

Allergy

Sustained anxieties, chronic fears, and associated chronic stresses, will exhaust the person. Then the immune system, which defends the body against invasion by disease, becomes depleted. A person can become so used to living with anxiety and stress that they fail to notice this occurring. The body will then react abnormally to any shock, even to a fairly slight shock like contact with an unaccustomed foreign substance. Whatever the shock was connected with (whether animal, vegetable or mineral) may thereafter cause allergy. Surface membranes at the interface between inside and outside – that is, both the external skin and the internal mucous membranes - react with a strange sort of inflammation. The depleted body will have been unable to make proper antibodies to defend itself against the particular invading foreign substance which the shock was connected with. So it will have done the next best thing, and histamine and other biological agents are released in an attempt to keep the offending object at bay. This can give rise to various sorts of allergic response, such as eczema, hay fever, asthma, even diarrhoea or fainting. Thus certain animals and plants, and various substances, including various foods, can trigger sudden allergy, with an associated exacerbation of fear, panic and stress. On rare occasions this may even be life-threatening, and require urgent medical treatment.

The root of the problem lies in the sort of chronic stress described in the last chapter (Chapter 4). The individual may not even be aware of the extent to which he or she is under strain. But the Lord will reveal it if he is asked to do so. And a demon of fear will need to be dealt with, as described above. Acknowledging Jesus and coming into the kingdom of God brings healing and relief.[35]

It is worth noting that similar mechanisms of chronic hidden stress and relative debilitation, followed by an abnormal immune response to infection by a bacterium, are found in tuberculosis.

Obsessions and compulsions (OCD)

Attention may occasionally be displaced away from deeper anxiety by stereotyped ritual behaviour.[36] Desperate ambivalence, or intolerable feelings that come from traumatic memories, or chronic fears, or distorted beliefs, may be kept at bay by compulsive rituals, such as hand washing, for example, or checking. The person often fears that something terrible might happen if the ritual is not performed. Sometimes obsessive thoughts may serve the same purpose by coming into the mind in stereotyped form, and although they may distress the person it may seem impossible to shake them off. Obsessions serve to control deeper issues that have seemed impossible to come to terms with. They may be triggered by a set of circumstances that consciously or unconsciously remind the person of the hidden underlying cause.

Fear and bitterness are often major parts of the problem, and demons of fear, unforgiveness, anger, etc., may need to be expelled in the name of Jesus. They may first need to be authoritatively bound up and rendered inactive whilst underlying facts are established and wounds are healed.

---

[35] Henry W. Wright deals with allergies at greater length in his book *A More Excellent Way*. I am in agreement with him.

[36] Displacement activity like this was first described in animals by Konrad Z. Lorenz in *King Solomon's Ring* (1950).

Tics

Tics (which are sudden jerks or compulsive utterances of one sort or another (including the so-called <u>Gilles de la Tourette syndrome</u>) are similar. The person will be chronically stressed, though often unwittingly so. And tics can usefully be regarded as compulsive displacement activity triggered when intolerance of anxiety becomes overwhelming.

For healing, it is necessary to meet Jesus and then open the heart to him personally in a very thorough way, allowing the Holy Spirit to open up the soul. It is necessary to be in a safe place with understanding people around, and to persevere in allowing memories to come up and be reconciled to God. This way past traumas and troubles and frightening events, may be exposed and healed by the Lord. So stress will be alleviated. It will be necessary, too, to expel demons as they become apparent. Demons of frustration, unworthiness, self-hatred, coprophilia and fear are common.

Sex addiction

The nature of the expression of a person's sexuality will usually seem to have been determined by the nature of a person's first genital sexual experience, which will inevitably be of abiding interest because it is always so all-consuming. Quite naturally, and sometimes quite unwittingly, there will have been a powerful desire to repeat it, whether it was actually pleasurable or not. The outcome can be very pleasurable if the first experience and the subsequent desire to repeat it is all worked out in marriage. Otherwise there will inevitably be frustrations, misunderstandings and rejections, with associated anxieties and stress, that all need healing.

All sorts of sexual temptations may be indulged in to assuage a person's anxieties and frustrations, including pornography, and masturbation with all sorts of fantasies, and sometimes with prostitutes, too. These temptations easily become obsessive. The compulsive drive to repeat sexual acts will cause addiction to be powerfully reinforced unless there is healing.[37] Masturbation with fantasy, furthermore, will reinforce a compulsion to enact the fantasy. There are plenty of people in prisons who wish they had never indulged such masturbatory fantasy.

Although this sort of behaviour is often simply accepted as normal and part of the personality, it will interfere with sexual enjoyment when a permanent partner is found. Although a person may assume they have self-control over their sexual interests and behaviour, this often proves not to be the case.

Many people are secretly driven by demonic lust. The origins are quite often to be found in childhood abuse of one sort or another. Early experiences of sexual seduction, abuse and perversion may underlie all sorts of other habitual patterns of behaviour, too, and cause trouble. Such experiences may require deep and confidential healing.

Unscrupulous people may notice some tendency that betrays the existence of sexual wounds and frustrations, and put temptation in a person's way in order to trap them. Initially the offer may seem very inviting, particularly because of a natural desire to repeat sexual experience. But a person's weakness can be used to exploit them. The result will be subtle intimidation, control, domination and eventual misery. Pimps control prostitutes this way, offering protection and control through fear, in the mistaken belief that what had happened to the prostitute in the past, to make her vulnerable to being trapped in sex work, can never be healed.

Who wants to be at the mercy of others (see 2 Samuel 24:14)? Surely it is better to be at the mercy of God to whom each one of us will have to give an account for their responses and actions despite everything that may have happened. Provided a safe-enough place, with safe-enough people, is available, a person may be healed in the name of Jesus through allowing all the facts

---

[37] See my section on Compulsive Repetition in Chapter 7 of *Healing for the Wounded Life.*

to be revealed in truth by the Holy Spirit, through applying the word of God, and through repentance and deliverance. This is the way repetitive patterns of behaviour can be broken. In the same sort of way Father God heals all sorts of other compulsions, too.

Asperger's syndrome

Prolonged severe anxiety and fear in a pregnant mother can sometimes instil such stress in the unborn child that instinctive communication between mother and child during the pregnancy is distorted. Stress and anxiety prevent both mother and child being sensitive to other matters. Stress and anxiety continue in the child after birth, becoming built in for life, and interfering with truthful perception unless there is healing.

Confusions and fears, and anger and rejection due to misunderstandings, lead the child both to fantasise about reality and also to tend to concentrate obsessively only on what seems of immediate concern. This frustrates development. The anxiety of uncertainty may seem so intolerably stressful that obsessional rituals become an habitual means of avoiding it. Loving and being loved may become difficult.

As the child grows, understanding of what is going on is frequently misconstrued and premature conclusions become strongholds of the mind that are aggressively defended. . "I have so much stress and anxiety I can't think straight," someone said. Episodes of stressful confusion may occasionally become psychotic.

A person with "Asperger's" may spend long periods of time compulsively involved in obsessions and have a very narrow, circumscribed field of interests, and be relatively clumsy and trust no one. In milder cases the certainties of measurement and scientific reason may displace the flexibility and good humour necessary to maintain interest in the give and take of personal relationships. Occasionally the person may seem too distracted by unhealed material below the surface of consciousness to be able to reach more than a cursory understanding of interpersonal relations.

But, as with autism (footnote 33), this person is made in God's image and can know the peace of God, and find healing, through accepting Jesus. Trouble during pregnancy, rejection in the womb, inherited grief, fear, curses, occultism, insecurity and anger, commonly play a major role in the development of this condition. There may, of course, have been many difficulties causing the mother's own stress. She may have had to make unpleasant compromises. Her relationships with her husband, perhaps, or with her extended family and others, and with God, may not always have been conducive to the spiritual well-being of her child. An understanding of this will be helpful, and it can all be laid on the Lord.

So the person must come into a place where people gather into the name of the Lord Jesus (Matthew 18:19-20). The process of demolishing strongholds of the mind, healing wounds of the soul and reactive sin, and perseverance in developing godly understanding of everyday events and relationships, may take a long time. It may be necessary to set firm boundaries and to insist that violence is forbidden. Demons will need expulsion at an appropriate time. They cannot remain in the person in the real presence of God.

Nevertheless it is worthwhile to persevere with taking every thought captive for Christ with kindness and patience. If the afflicted person will allow and accept what Jesus accomplished on the cross, healing becomes possible.

Anorexia nervosa

Like many other medical labels, anorexia nervosa is simply a description in Latin that sounds as though scientific doctors have the condition beaten. Labels like this are good for trade, but they also serve to make the condition the sole preserve of the medical profession, which need not be the case. In translation, the term just means "not eating for nervous reasons."

Most orthodox psychiatrists see anorexia nervosa as an obsessive dread of fatness. Weight loss may indeed occasionally become so severe as to lead to death. And when it is this severe there is no option but to involve the doctors.

Bulimia (Greek 'boulimia' = ravenous hunger) may be associated with it, in which case overeating is associated with vomiting and purging in order to control the weight. These are classified as "eating disorders."

The most usual way for doctors, nurses and psychologists to attempt to manage these conditions is by supportive psychotherapy, trying to give encouragement, and trying to maintain nutrition by persuasion. Occasionally there may be some attempt to discover reasons why such a pattern of behaviour should have taken hold.

To get out of it you have to get into it. If the person will come to Jesus and accept him as saviour and meekly allow the Holy Spirit to bring relevant issues to light, it will be found that, for real healing to come, serious difficulties in relationships with familiar people need to be changed. The real presence of Jesus in a person's life makes it possible for truth to be faced so that cover-up is no longer necessary.[38] An anorexic person may silently be screaming, "I am not ready to grow up yet!" And there may be too much unresolved, unfinished business for the person to swallow anything more. Such issues are very sensitive, and Jesus is the only person with sufficient authority to make it possible for them to be fully addressed and healed.

Look at it this way, for example. You cannot eat with people who manipulate you without acknowledging it, and who consequently infuriate you, but whom you also want to love. You may feel you owe them all sorts of conflicting obligations. You

---

[38] Personal truth grows through never betraying Jesus who redeemed you with his blood. But you cannot expect other people, even those closest to you, fully to respect this. Therefore you need wisdom from the Holy Spirit to know how to act and speak with them.

will be aware that they are your security, especially because you are becoming weak. You cannot eat with people who turn your deep concerns back on you by accusing you, often through innuendo, whilst denying that they do so. You may be able to see their defences but they are in the majority and a lot depends on their defences being maintained. So what chance do you have? It seems you cannot win! Whenever there is an opening to eat, you may overindulge in desperation, longing for comfort, and then vomit. The situation makes you sick because there seems no redress for you other than this wretchedness. Indeed, you may have an unconscious desire to vomit all over them. Otherwise you might wilt away. But then you would remain secretly angry and wounded.

It might be possible to take some food if you will forgive them, although the trauma they inflict on your soul will continue until they change, or until you die, or until you become strong enough in the Lord to deal with them, or until you find some way of getting out of the situation without taking them with you. After all, those people have always been significant and important for you, they are part of you, but you desperately need a break from them. But then who else will look after you? Where else can you go?

Unspeakable dynamics will be found to have contributed to this terrible, stubborn obsession. It is necessary not only to forgive but also to be willing to do so constantly. It is also necessary to stand up for yourself with the Lord's help. This will involve addressing your crushed spirit and your false guilt, also your anger and hostility, and your shame, and your sense of rejection and your sense of self-hatred, and probably your jealousy and ambivalence and a few other matters that the Lord will show you, too. But first it will be necessary to discover something of the truth of what has been going on. And if you find anyone to help you address all these issues, most certainly it is worth persevering together for as long as it takes, or at least as long as possible, even if you discover that those willing to help you have their own imperfections, too.

Father God is the one who will actually be setting you free, and most certainly he wants to do so. He sent Jesus, his only begotten son, to die for you, who paid the price to redeem you. Jesus overcame all the powers of death and destruction and rose from the dead, and is alive and wants you in his kingdom, so you don't need to despair. No one who turned to him for healing failed to be healed. By his Spirit he will show you every detail of how to overcome with that same resurrection power. So put yourself into his hands and persist with a humble heart in asking him to show you your way to the God who heals. Luke 18:1-8 may be relevant.

6

DEPRESSION AND MANIA

Secular view

When a person feels miserable for too long, and can't shake it off, and starts to imagine something may be wrong, a medical doctor is often consulted. Commonly this results in the prescription of an antidepressant drug. In the UK about one person in ten is taking an antidepressant drug. Despair and melancholy have become medicalized. Most people see them as a medical illness needing treatment. Medical language is now used to speak about them.

Textbooks used for medical diagnosis describe 'depression' in terms of low mood, reduced energy, little or no capacity for enjoyment, lack of interest, poor concentration, agitation, disturbed appetite and sleep, a sense of worthlessness, and so on. In 'severe depression' they include suicidal ideas or attempts at suicide, physical complaints, delusions, hallucinations, silent stuporous misery, and self-starvation.

If the person suffers not only episodes of low mood with decreased energy but also periodic episodes of elevated mood with increased energy the medical textbooks diagnose the condition as 'bipolar affective disorder', or 'manic depression' (which is the older term).

Manic behaviour may sometimes become dangerous, due to excitability, grossly elated mood, loss of social inhibitions, over-familiarity, and lack of self-control, resulting in serious irresponsibility, gross hyperactivity, loss of money and property, violence, inappropriate sexual liaisons, decreased need for sleep, and persistent garrulousness that may become utterly unintelligible. If this sort of behaviour is excessive but not totally gross it is called 'hypomania'. And if it is appallingly gross it is called 'mania', and emergency services will be necessary forcibly to stop the deluded, manic person from continuing to cause havoc. Such extravagant extremes of mood may occasionally be isolated, but more often they are recurrent. They should be considered likely to recur unless there is healing for the root causes. Of course it is entirely appropriate for medical specialists to be involved in the acute management of such emergencies.

Secular psychiatry

Psychiatry as usually practised is mostly about managing illness and controlling symptoms, often using drugs, psychological techniques or hospitalisation. Very occasionally a psychiatrist may recommend a talking cure or a psychotherapist.

If a distressed and disturbing person should become an unmanageable danger to himself or herself, it will of course be necessary to take that person to a place of safety, which is often a hospital, and to attempt some sort of first aid. More radical cure will always take time, because deep issues will need to be addressed and personal change effected.

If secular psychological techniques are used, they generally work by exposing significant issues, and by then applying carrot and stick incentives to try to correct supposedly harmful behaviour. More appropriate behaviour will then be reinforced, often by inducing a fear of backsliding. From an Arminian Christian[39] point of view the trouble with such techniques is as Paul says in Romans 7:15, "...what I want to do I do not do." Unless the heart is changed the person does not essentially

---

[39] Amongst Calvinists and so -called 'reformed' Christians it is common to find preaching and teaching about the ideals of how Christians should behave and live, with the assumption that God will enable conformity to the ideal after a person accepts Jesus as saviour and Lord. They fail to realise that the heart takes time to develop understanding and needs other people for love and empathetic encouragement. So the result is a legalism that works the same way as secular psychology.

change, so will probably relapse.

Change of heart comes about through opening your heart with someone, then effectively giving your heart to a spiritual being who has the power and authority of a god. It is necessary to allow your spiritual allegiance to affect the parts and aspects of your body and soul so as to bring healing. And the only god I trust to do this is the living God who sent his only begotten son to redeem me. Unless the heart is changed this way, the mind and the will continue to work in the same old way. They can be manipulated, but they are not free, and further trouble may ensue in consequence.[40]

When a diagnosis is given and drugs are prescribed, however, there comes a sense that at least someone with authority knows what is going on and seems willing to help. This can be a great relief. An anxious, stressed, depressed person becomes calmer. The drugs take effect and make the person feel safer, less distressed and less distressing to others.

But the apparent peace obtained from drugs is an illusion, because it leaves deep-seated issues unhealed and depends on a regular supply of the medication. Drugs used to treat depression simply correct the biochemical concomitants of natural responses, so as to make the physiology seem more or less unemotional, and thus make the person feel more stable. Psychotropic drugs are manufactured cushions against true reality.

Nevertheless, psychotropic drugs may be used to hold a person in a tolerable condition until faith builds up and true healing becomes possible. Since there is so much misery, and since most people have no living faith, public health considerations make it necessary to control people with drugs to prevent civil unrest. Health services help keep the peace; but by mollifying their misery psychotropic drugs enable people to dwell in some degree of unreality.

---

[40] Thomas Aquinas would not have agreed with me; but Duns Scotus would have understood.

Making connections and discovering meaning

Many people become worried if how they feel seems perhaps to be abnormal. They should not worry too much, however, because it is a fact that in many cases a modicum of healing may come without any special help at all, particularly if the person will listen to their body and ask God for sufficient understanding. God has built healing mechanisms into our physiology, and drugs are often unnecessary. Surely a person can be allowed to be sad!

It is common, however, for a depressed person not to understand why they should have become so wretched or what triggers the mood swings. Yet full insight is not always a necessary prerequisite for a fair measure of healing, and sometimes people just need time and space to catch up with themselves, time for reflection, or sufficient 'drifting' time, like the time between sleeping and waking. Things come to mind during such dreamy times, and connections are often made that are sufficiently healing. Thus with sufficient rest healing may come, often with some degree of insight and understanding.

Many people who actually break down cannot figure out enough of the reason why they should feel so bad. They really cannot say why they are depressed, nor can they qualify their depression very much at all. And the existential details will differ from one person to another. It is not possible to put everyone's depression down to one or two common antecedents. It is commonly acknowledged that everyone's depression is different in the details.

The use of the word "depression" in everyday English, moreover, is not precise. The term is used for a multitude of conditions that in other languages are described more meaningfully using more particular nouns. English is the only language that uses 'depression' as a blanket term to cover a multitude of mental, emotional and physical states. It would help us understand the condition better if we were to become more familiar with such universal concepts as alienation, discouragement, despondency, dejection, despair, grief, hopelessness, hypochondria, oppression, sadness, weariness, ennui, anhedonia, stress, misery, melancholy, rejection, restlessness, torture, trauma, torment, wretchedness, and even "the blues". Further qualifications can be found to make the description fit each afflicted individual even more accurately.

One person may become depressed through circumstances that would not trouble another, too. Bereavement may be a major factor in one person's depression, overwork in that of another, repressed guilt and self-blame in that of another, chronic frustration, anger or jealousy in that of another, alcohol abuse in another, and so on.

A sense of loss, insignificance, emptiness, unworthiness, worthlessness, loneliness, or horror may come upon a person as wounds, perhaps of uncertain origin, fester in the soul. Wounds may be more keenly felt as they are coming into awareness. But awareness is often suppressed for fear of becoming overwhelmed. There may be wounds of rejection, frustration, pain, abandonment. There may be wounds from the loss of attachment. There may be wounds of loneliness, sadness, anger. The more chaotic the torment is, the more withdrawn the person may become and then, in consequence, the more rejected and dejected. The emotional pain can sometimes become so terrible that even holding oneself together sufficiently to cope with the simple details of toilet and food may eventually become exhaustingly stressful.

You have no energy, no interest; you tend to weep, or maybe you are just too sad for tears; you avoid other people; you are tired but restless, you cannot sleep, then after sleep eventually comes you awaken far too soon, conscious of stress and tormenting thoughts and dreams; you eat too much, or perhaps too little; you neglect yourself; nothing seems to provide any enjoyment whatever. There seems no hope and no point. You no longer have any courage, and your energy has been sapped. You lose sound judgement so that other people easily exploit you, and in consequence you may feel vulnerable, terrified, even paranoid and suspicious of deception where there is none. You may have given up altogether and just lie in bed, restless, apathetic, silent, unable to go on.

Beneath such wretchedness there may be a lot of frustration. There may be bottled up anger, resentment, horror, hatred, violence. There may be rejection, hurt, misunderstanding, worry. There may be disappointment, discouragement, despair, hopelessness. There may be loss, grief, mourning. There may be loneliness. There may be wounds of abuse and neglect so bad that your will power may seem to have been utterly destroyed. Someone else may have been subtly telling you what to think or what to do, more or less directing your life, dominating you, or even cursing you. There may be guilt you do not know what to do with. There may be lies and deception. There may be demons. Depression and wretchedness may have run in the family. There may be serious sin inherited from ancestors. Ways of coping will inevitably have been inherited, along with attitudes and prejudices that may be unhelpful, obscuring God's light. Confusion may be so bad that nothing has much meaning. There may be a lot of personal mistakes that you would rather not call sin or acknowledge to be wrong with God.

Until God's love and mercy and power to heal is known, there is naturally a great reluctance to admit that things you have been involved with and done may be hated by God. Then again, some things that you feel bad about may not in fact be wrong with God at all, and some of the guilt that oppresses you may be quite unnecessary. There may be a silent scream. Or you may be too stressed and utterly worn out even to muster the energy to panic.

Out of the dark
Because you have never described how you are feeling in detail to someone who understands, and have never spoken about the salient issues connected with those feelings, you have

113

never understood your condition in any depth. You have never opened up what may lie in the dark. You have not allowed light to be shed on it. This could have prevented you from finding a way out of it. Of course it can seem intolerable to dwell upon loss or grief or dread, overwhelming hopelessness, nothingness, emptiness, black despair, total loss of energy, and so on. But a beginning may be made if there is someone who can understand without reacting, someone who can somehow help contain it, someone with credible empathy. Even if you cannot trust other people with it, you can trust God. And it may be worth trusting other people who are humble enough to put their trust in God, and mature enough to wait on him for guidance.

Neither public sector services nor private insurance companies will pay for the time this sort of thing takes, however. Actuarial calculations cannot properly be applied to the relationships. To them it is cheaper to prescribe medication. The state will not take responsibility for the various different spiritual pathways used for understanding and responding to human distress. They fear that litigation, in a society with many faiths, could pose too challenging a burden and expense.

Many people who have become depressed have been trying, often unconsciously, to let other people know what has been going on for them, only to discover that they have not been truly understood and have instead been diagnosed. Indeed, their very symptoms and their body language will have contained a message. But no one was willing or able to articulate with it well enough. Although what was being communicated by their person in this way may have had profound significance and urgency, it was not possible to bring it fully into the light – all that was possible, maybe, was groans (as in Romans 8:22-23). A person may need the sound-enough empathy of other people to put what is truly on their heart into adequate expression before God.

The reason the truth of experience has not been able to be admitted in this way may be that other people would not, or could not, hear. They could or would not perceive the truth of what was going on. So they may have effectively dismissed you without having really meant to do so. Such experience may have made you imagine that what you said may have been mistaken, crazy, invalid, or even mad. Such perceived rejection can, indeed, make a person into a psychiatric invalid. Rejection like this can be a serious trauma, particularly if it is accompanied by the curse of a diagnosis. It will be very necessary, for the sake of your own healing, to forgive all the people who have been so ignorant as to judge you in this way.

If it should never have seemed necessary, or possible, to be reconciled to God about such issues, a person may have become so lost and alienated as to have been visiting psychiatric wards and clinics for years, sometimes with many sessions of electroconvulsive therapy (ECT), or injections of medication that hold you chemically in frustrated rigidity. Hopelessness may then be profound, although medical treatment may camouflage it. By the grace of God depression is not always as bad as this, but it can certainly sometimes be utterly dreadful.

How can you speak about what may underlie your wretchedness and depression if everyone you have ever known has been anxious or worried or angry or dismissive about what you said, or has just tried to impose their own solutions upon you?

Some people have believed they might die if they tell, and sometimes they may indeed have things to tell that other people have warned them never to tell on pain of death. In such a case, how can you ever make someone else understand what you are suffering?

How oppressive it is to have to exclude so much of what is deep in your heart from the company you keep! Why did you lose your voice? What is the pressure pushing you down, and "depressing" you? What has been going on for this to be so dreadfully the case, despite our actually being made in the image of God?

If details of the experience of depression begin meaningfully to be spoken about by the sufferer, however, and true connections are made with past and present facts and events, it may begin to become apparent that what was first considered to be a medical illness is being transformed into an understandable human reaction.

Sometimes it takes a long time before there is a glimmer of light. Sometimes words will eventually come through the use of pre-verbal paint, or creative play, or drama, or music. It will always be worth persevering to bring what is unknown in your darkness into the light. Eventually truth becomes apparent, with healing if you will come into the presence of almighty God and accept the victory the Lord Jesus Christ won on the cross over the death and destruction which is trying to win. Jesus is the light for the world. He has already won the battle.

God is quite capable of addressing you directly, if ever you give him the opportunity. But connecting with another human being, who is willing genuinely and patiently to attend to how you truly are, can often be the real beginning of healing. Together with such a person, insight and healing from God may come to you, provided you use what passes between you actually to listen to God in the name of Jesus.

People need people. They also need God.

Validation

From the earliest moments of a person's life it is necessary for the experiences of the individual to be validated by other people. This assumes the common grace of God and some awareness of truth. Otherwise there may be misperception, misunderstanding, miscommunication, insecurity, confusion, frustration, fear, and so on. The first person to whom you effectively give account is your mother, and the process of giving and taking account with each other actually begins intuitively in the womb.

It is important for a mother to take every aspect of her baby's communication and complaint seriously and to engage in

116

conversation about all of it with her child. And the mother needs to be able to take her concerns to her husband, and be sufficiently understood to have his real protection. Many other significant people will count, too. What they think and feel will influence the growing child profoundly, through the mother.

To have people to whom to give your ongoing narrative account, and from whom to receive godly opinions, enables matters to come to light that can be processed within the soul from earliest days to build maturity. Those people are fortunate who are able to continue this process from the womb into childhood, then with increasing sophistication into adolescence, adulthood and old age. We are social beings, and the more we sort out and put right with God in this world, with each other's help, the better will be our resurrection in the next (Matthew 25:14-30, Hebrews 11:35). One day each one of us shall have to give our individual account personally to God (note Romans 2:16, 5:13, 10:14, 14:12, and Hebrews 4:16, etc.).

When there has not been sufficiently open discussion of salient issues within a family, there will be some degree of insecurity in the child. The wool will have been pulled over the child's eyes, as it were, concerning various questions. Such insecurity can make it difficult to find words and develop mature understanding when you are older. In adolescence and youth unresolved issues from early childhood often reappear time and time again, one way or another, until they can eventually be brought into the light, and talked through and reconciled to God and healed. Significant experiences during adolescence and youthful years, when so much is still being learned, have lasting effects upon a person, and these, too, need to be brought into the light, reconciled to God and healed. It helps to have no restrictions on what may be discussed in families – including the family of God's kingdom. The church family is often called upon to provide care and safety for people seeking healing for wounds incurred in their original families.

When a mother fears God, cares for her children wisely, discusses things openly and is herself a strong example of righteousness, her children will be strong and resilient, even if there is poverty and even if circumstances are distressing. When the hearts of fathers turn to their children, and children to their fathers, as God desires (Malachi 4:6), mothers are free to educate children intelligently.

Of course, not every period of wretchedness and depression has its origin in the most formative years. But, when you really enquire into it, a surprising amount of later trouble will be found to originate there.

Sadly, the fear of God is often lost when circumstances become difficult. Furthermore, true causes of distress are often not explained to children or openly discussed for the children to make up their own minds. Scripture advises us not to exasperate our children (Ephesians 6:4). People easily lose hope and impose their own solutions, and dominate, and manipulate, and control the situation, and fail to seek God's help and wait for it. In consequence, relationships may become unrighteous and events may not work out so well. Then stress becomes further compounded by efforts to put things right in human strength alone in order to keep on going. As mistakes and wounds are covered up, all sorts of deals and compromises are made for the sake of respectable appearance or expediency. Both internal and external stresses become worse, and actual illness may supervene, because God's peace has been lost.

Secular counselling and psychotherapy

Counsellors and psychotherapists specialise in listening with discernment, and in providing a safe place for painful issues to be addressed. But the quality of their discernment depends not only upon the thoroughness with which their training has been effective in sorting out their own issues but also upon their spiritual allegiance (although few would acknowledge this).

The difference between counsellors and psychotherapists is subtle but significant. Both will have received a training in which they will have applied to their own lives the system of thinking and the beliefs they now profess. A counsellor will be applying theoretical teaching. A psychotherapist, however, will be allowing you to become attached to some degree to his or her person whilst nurturing you through a process of working free. The affairs of the heart are analysed in various ways, depending on the belief system of the psychotherapist, in order to achieve this.

A modern version of psychotherapy, which may be available briefly and without charge in countries that have a free health service, is Cognitive Behavioural Therapy, which involves detailed practical investigation of your predicament, and limited personal encouragement to find steps out of it. The ethos is usually secular and humanistic and the effects may not be profound or long lasting, although they may be enough to effect some change for the better.

Depression will often initially have been triggered by events that actually bear some similarity to past events which gave rise to unhealed issues. When relationships go wrong, and the reason is not clear, and the emotion and distress being felt is out of proportion to what has recently occurred, the cause may be that recent events have triggered memory of events in the past that have not really been healed. You may have been unconsciously reminded, by similar circumstances, of what requires sorting out. Furthermore, you may have been compensating for unhealed mistakes and problems of the past by behaviour which has become habitual, but which stresses you, because it is inherently a counterbalance.

For example, a man had not realised that a woman, with whom he had in the past done many good business deals, reminded him of his dead mother. One day, however, she unexpectedly reneged on an important agreement, and betrayed him so badly that he lost a very substantial sum of money. This triggered severe, chronically recurrent depression, for which he received extensive psychiatric treatment. Only later did it dawn upon him that his depression was essentially related to many unresolved issues that still complicated his grief concerning his mother's death.

Because medication seemed to interfere with the alertness of his mind and his work, his doctor eventually sent him to see a female psychoanalytic psychotherapist, whom he visited regularly and paid privately for several years. Significant issues from the past became apparent as the professional relationship with the psychotherapist developed. The relationship with his mother came under scrutiny because it seemed a powerful influence on his relationship with the therapist herself who, he eventually realised, also reminded him of his mother. The therapist was sensitive to how he saw her, and they were able to speak about this transference in detail. In consequence he began to find healing for his grief.

It is in this sort of way that a psychotherapist can hold you through your trouble as you work through the relevant issues.

Unlike counselling, psychotherapy is not, strictly speaking, active treatment. In psychotherapy you are not being indoctrinated or subjected to any sort of didacticism. Although you are free to leave the relationship at any time, it soon becomes clear that it is rather short sighted to leave just because of unpleasant or negative feelings. The therapist attends to you, and to what is going on, and helps you to be accountable for yourself particularly in respect of hidden issues. This could, and perhaps should, be construed simply as the sort of conversation a pastor may have with a suppliant (Proverbs 20:5). Any personal dependency upon a pastor or therapist can be useful, and need not be interminable. And it should be remembered that Paul recommends the suppliant to share all good things with the guide (Galatians 6:6, 2 Timothy 2:6).

Peace and healing from God

Most people in the helping professions, including doctors and nurses and psychologists and psychotherapists and counsellors, are not disciples of the Lord Jesus. Therefore personal resolution of issues will often be incomplete through not being reconciled to God. It is often the case, however, that disturbing matters are only clarified when they are spoken about with other people who are capable of sufficient compassion and understanding.

If you are a Christian you can sometimes work through your difficulties more efficiently than people who do not know the Lord, even when the help you are receiving is secular, because you can take all issues personally to God in the name of Jesus and receive supernatural revelation and healing (1 Peter 5:7).

If by good fortune the person you turn to for help is actually a follower of the Lord Jesus, it may well be that you have been effectively introduced to the Lord. In this case, discipleship should be openly transferred to the Lord by both of you. And of course your discipleship with the Lord should never be terminated, although discipleship with your mentor will be.

Many personal issues are complex, and there are many places in the Bible where people are encouraged to help one another with issues that may not be obvious (Leviticus 19:18, Luke 10:27, Proverbs 24:5-6, Galatians 6:1-5, James 5:16, Philippians 2:4, 1 Peter 5 2). Other trustworthy people are often necessary for true repentance and healing.

When two or three come together into the name of Jesus, and the Holy Spirit is present and people listen to him, truth will become apparent, and it will be possible for issues to be reconciled to God so that healing may be received through the presence of Jesus.

The peace of God comes from bringing all relevant matters into the light and being reconciled to God about them. Then God gives strength as you quietly put your trust in him. Isaiah 30:15 says, "In repentance and rest is your salvation." Yet often a person can only get to this point through being heard in such a way that what is being said is reflected back in a kindly way, so that the person begins to hear him- or her-self and to know and take account of what he or she is really saying. Only then can the person both give a proper account, and also take account before God.

Whether or not your account is adequate for healing will depend both upon the discernment of person who hears and also upon whether or not the Holy Spirit is present to bring you into all truth (John 16:13). So it is necessary to have a humble heart and to be forgiving towards any apparent inadequacies in the people you are finding it necessary to trust. And it is best to trust people with sufficient maturity, if you can find them.

Most of the best people to trust will have been through their own hell and wretchedness and will know about their own healing. And they will have the humility not to believe they know all the answers for you. Hopefully they will know the Lord, and be able to wait on him with you. But they are not always church leaders or professionals; although occasionally they may be.

Things not put right with God often hark right back to childhood – or even before. Whenever you have had to retain emotions and thoughts in your heart instead of admitting them to the light, those things remain hidden in unconscious memory in your living body. Your body can, in this sense, be likened to a room full of unknown secret things. The way in - the door - is the way out. It is necessary to allow yourself to connect with your body and discover what is in there, and bring it before the Lord. It all needs to be brought into the light and remembered and yielded to God in the name of Jesus for you to be free.

When you present your body as a living sacrifice to God, thanking him for Jesus and praising him, he will renew your mind. Through love he will change it all so that it conforms to his will (Romans 12:1-2).

Then you must allow yourself to receive God's healing in your body. Habits and reflexes change, even the physiology will change in some respects. God even knows what happened when you were carried in your mother's womb. He even heals the genes.

The process may take time and it is greatly helped if other Christians accept your experience as you relate it. It helps if they make no demands except that you allow them to encourage you in the truth. And if they are willing and able to be generously hospitable, especially when you are feeling terrible, it is a real bonus and blessing.

Criticism

There are limits to this, of course. If you take no account of how they are affected by you, and just dump your misery without taking responsibility for it, you should expect their criticism. Mind you, criticism can be constructive, particularly if it is backed by Scripture (2 Timothy 3:16, 2:25, 4:2, Titus 2:15, 2 Peter 3:9,) and if you accept that it is the word of your loving God, and therefore listen to it.

Christians are allowed to exercise judgement in respect of others (1 Corinthians 5 and 6). But they do not have authority to condemn (see Matthew 5:22 and 7:1-5, also Romans 8:1-2). Slander (Proverbs 30:10), cursing (Psalm 109) and grumbling (James 5:9) are to be avoided. But criticism need not be condemnation. It may usefully lead to discussion and debate (see Acts 15 and 19). People who are extra-sensitive to criticism may need to repent of self-condemnation or pride. When you listen with God to what other people say about how you affect them, you may realise that those other people actually care about you and that you can travel together honestly through whatever may be necessary in order to find healing.

This is a good way to make repentance in detail. It not only brings healing but also enables sanctification and maturity to be built into character. People do not find true healing through being told to be different, nor through human reasoning, but rather through revelation from Holy Spirit as they engage their hearts in true fellowship with each other in the presence of the Lord. But the revelation is not always pleasant. By opening up matters that are real (the hidden facts of real personal experience) and giving a true account without trying to be good or to obey religious rules, a person may open sufficiently to receive God's light.

God reveals himself through his creation (Romans 1:20), through his word (Psalm 119:105, John 1:1-5) and also amongst his people (Matthew 18:20). His presence (Luke 5:17) and his word (Proverbs 4:20-22) are healing. They are at hand to be received. The heart and the mind will tend to come into conformity with the person of God once He dwells with a person. The Holy Spirit will be in charge of the process, and bring healing and wholeness if you genuinely bring everything discovered through your relationships into the light, and reconcile it all to God through the cross of Jesus.

We people were originally created in the image of God, but we have not been faithful to his love. We have failed to hold to the truth of his word. We have perverted his designs. The potential is still present in each individual, nevertheless, to follow him and become righteous through personally accepting the victory won by his only begotten son Jesus on the cross, and receiving Holy Spirit. This is not fanciful but real. Our godless past need not dictate the future. God is able to make all things new.

The sort of issues that may come up

We are made in God's image, and living according to our maker's instructions brings peace. But if personal relationships and actions have been wrong according to the word of God, some degree of basic anxiety and stress will naturally have been generated within the soul and body. Every one of us is a sinner who has fallen short of the glory of God (Romans 3:23) and God has mercy on those who fear him (Luke 1:50). And he encourages us to love our neighbours as ourselves.

At a time of trial or trouble, anguish or despair, if God's guidance has not been sought and the person has given in to wild emotion, and there has been no real understanding from other

124

people, many deceptive ways of thinking, and demons, may unwittingly have been adopted. If a disappointed person has given in to misery, self-pity or hopelessness, blaming, envying, judging or cursing others, the only light they will have will be that of their own reason, and their only recompense some sort of retaliation. When the victory won by Jesus on the cross is left out of the equation healing is never complete. A sense of boredom and cynicism may result, with bitterness, irritability and envy. Rejection by others may be expected, and a sense of abandonment, exclusion, and irrelevance can develop quite naturally. A person can become tormented by this sort of thing.

Cruelty, torture, rape, and violence, naturally lead to chronic states of anxiety and insecurity, fear, confusion and unreality. Hatred, shame, guilt and rejection, and unwillingness to forgive, naturally lead to callousness. As a result, some may have murdered, stolen, prostituted themselves, abused themselves with drugs, been members of gangs or secret societies, lied, extorted, betrayed others, manipulated, indulged all sorts of sexual desires and fantasies, lived for self-gratification without thought for others, and so on. Relationships will be distorted by guilt, shame, resentment, wounds. The chronic stresses can lead to profound misery. The past always catches up with us.

Frustration, anger and confusion may come from lack of understanding and rejection by others, or perhaps from wounds of failure. Loneliness may crush the spirit. Some people may never have been able to love anyone without being abused. Some people may never have been able to believe it could be better to have loved and lost than never to have loved at all. And so on. The devil specialises in every subtle form of trauma and deception. And every member of this fallen human race is capable of being a monster. Depressions can be the result.

Or it may seem that many wrong decisions have been taken that now seem impossible to repair. For instance, a person may be regretting having had an abortion. Abortions are usually far more traumatic than is commonly assumed. Or a person may have been living under some sort of slavery, domination, worry or oppression for years. It may have been impossible to escape from overpowering wickedness

Or events that were acceptable at the time may now be seen in a different light. The pain of a broken home may at last be being realised.

Wounds of bereavement and loss, of injustice, of violence, of being rejected, or of being effectively cursed, can cause long lasting oppression, and misery and fear. Complicated secrets and ties to other people, which may be the result of past sexual liaisons or of spiritual commitments, covenants, curses or vows, the full details of which are often hidden from people who have been ensnared by them, can generate fatigue and exhaustion as time goes on, with the torment of seeming to have no time, no peace, no real rest. Physical illness may even develop in consequence. That, too, can make you chronically miserable.

Worse still, perhaps, shock and fear may have come into your body through experiences that have been physically traumatic, violent, and appalling. They may have made you very frightened and confused. And there may be a reluctance to recall such traumatic events for fear of re-living them.

Suicide

Many people have been tempted to commit suicide as a way out. But there is nothing in the Bible that indicates that death will save you. The act of suicide is a rejection of the saving grace and power of God. It is done in unbelief. According to the Bible we should expect it to be judged severely (1 Corinthians 3:16-17). Furthermore it is experienced as a curse by those connected with you. Many people will be wounded if you do this, and some will struggle to forgive you.

Healing

The process of healing involves coming into the presence of God, discovering the truth with the help of the Holy Spirit, forgiving those who have offended you, receiving God's forgiveness for your own sin, and expelling any demons in the name of Jesus by the power of Holy Spirit. It is a step by step process, and it is impossible to set time limits.

The process of bringing everything out can sometimes be turbulent. Certain things may not be able to be said in certain company. There may be strong natural resistance to remembering until the person can be fairly sure of not being further traumatized if there should be confusion or any cathartic release of emotion. Then more memories may come to the surface. God knows it all.

When what you are suffering is opened up to the light of Jesus and met by other people with the Lord's understanding, your distress will be contained sufficiently through hospitable personal relationships for the Holy Spirit to do his work of healing. But it is unlikely that you will feel completely better straight away; and most probably you will feel dreadful. But you cannot trust your feelings. What is required is to persevere and endure the process of healing for as long as it takes, which may sometimes be a long time - a year or two, or even longer.

Circumstances conducive to healing

If people are not met in sincerity and truth in the Lord, if they have to be careful what they say or feel obliged to put on a good face and hide how they really are, very significant matters may never have the opportunity to come to light for the Lord's healing. People who stay like this often have long-term suffering. This is one reason why there are so many sick people in churches.

Depression is an increasingly common experience. The incidence seems to have increased as the incidence of genuine Christian faith in our society has declined.

Church programmes that have all the politically correct safeguards in place actually tend to make it unsafe for a person to move freely into truthful remembering with eventual healing, because routine programmes tend to put a person through a rather mechanical learning process whereby external controls impose other people's rationality and respectability without allowing a person sufficient time and space to give personal meaning to what is supposed to be learned. It is necessary to give meaning to the word of God in your life, to inwardly digest it whilst retaining freedom of speech and action, in order to make it real for yourself. Rules and legalism are not conducive to true healing. Openly sincere and truthful relationships in the Lord are what are necessary. Only then will genuine self-control develop as a fruit of the indwelling Spirit (Romans 12:9-21).

Some church elders who have gone through this sort of process of healing and sanctification for themselves might, perhaps, become skilled at facilitating groups of Christians sorting their lives out together. In order both to bear the pain of other people's suffering and also at the same time to hear what God is saying (as Jesus requires, note Matthew 13:16, Mark 4:21-25 and Luke 10:37), it is necessary to have allowed the word of God to take root in your own soul through what you yourself have been through and suffered. Mature understanding and personal holiness develop this way. Those who have been there know. Such true empathy helps others find healing. It takes people who have already been along the path themselves to help others gently to find their way (Hebrews 2:14). And groups led by such individuals can often help more people most effectively, with the added benefit of lasting fellowship.

Leaders in healing work will also need to understand spiritual warfare (1 Timothy 3, Titus 1:6-9). And those in authority should be under the Lord's authority, and have the meekness and gentleness of Christ (2 Corinthians 10:1). They will need to be able to minister deliverance when appropriate. And intercessors will be needed as watchmen. With these conditions, space will be created for people to open up their pain in the presence of God. Then the very deepest personal disturbances can be healed.

Because it has become impossible for this sort of godly healing work to be done in secular health services, nowadays the necessary conditions need to be available within churches, as part of a developing Christian culture that differs from the humanistic culture of the secular world. It may be that this is the real work of deacons. Many more people are needed for it.

One or two singular conditions should now be mentioned.

Post-natal depression

It is astonishing to realise how many women there are whose post-natal depression may be connected with bad experiences of childbirth, particularly with lack of personal understanding and compassion in the practice of scientific obstetrics. Many women may need to become willing to forgive their medical attendants or other influential people, so that God may begin to heal their trauma and distress.

Chronic fatigue (M.E.)

The so-called chronic fatigue syndrome ('myalgic encephalomyelitis', or "M.E.") is another way of suffering from chronic stresses. The physical body is chronically tired and has often been acutely stressed by a physical illness. There is a longing for greater rest - almost for an intrauterine state. But before true peace and rest can be found there are matters that will need to be allowed to come to mind through the work of the Holy Spirit, and then be reconciled to God. You have to work out before God what the chronic stress was which caused an acute stress to be so devastating. There are both physical and spiritual components to this condition, and the Lord heals both together. So you will need to ask the Lord to replenish your strength. And you will need to look inside your own soul and be willing to ask the Lord to assist your repentance so that you may change.

If any sort of domination has been crushing the spirit, you will need to allow God to make you aware of it. Any feeling of being wearied, imprisoned, trapped, or restricted by others frequently goes right back into childhood. You are likely, however, to find yourself caught with similar people and similar dynamics in the present, too.

So your issues will not only involve people from the past but also people you love and are closely involved with now in the present. And the folk around you may not be able to alter the way you feel. Although you may need to have some frank and difficult exchanges with those with whom you dwell, it is unlikely that you'll sort everything out with the people you live amongst for fear of painful misunderstandings. So they will only be able to watch you suffer, and they too will suffer because of your demands, which can make you feel worse. The fatigue itself is exhausting. The stress for everyone will be considerable. You may need to find help and encouragement from outside your normal circle of friends.

Habitual ways of coping with various issues will probably have been inherited. The sins of ancestors may need to be forgiven before present relationships can be corrected. Both you and those you live with and love may be found to have transferred relationships from the past into the present, so that relationships now actually have an oppressive quality. You will need to cut yourself free in the name of Jesus from wrong relationships and soul ties past and present, and break any curses, and forgive and bless those who may have cursed you either in the present generation or through past generations. You may also have to confess wrong worship engaged in by ancestors.

You will need to confess any guilt you have, both real and false, and be forgiven for your fears and insecurities. Shock may need the Lord's healing. Ambivalence, frustration, anger, hidden rage, despair and hopelessness, defeat and denials, may need to be confessed and healed. You may have to order demons out of you in Jesus name.

There is a deep conversation you need to have with God in the name of Jesus. Search your heart on your bed (Psalm 4:4). Find someone to trust who will not take advantage of you and allow yourself to speak openly and pay attention to what you find yourself saying and thinking about. Allow the Holy Spirit to expose what needs to change, and make yourself accountable to God. It will probably take some time. Allow it!

Bipolar disorder (hypomania and mania)

Occasionally a person may become acutely overactive and overexcited, high as a kite, losing self-control and perhaps seeming to talk gibberish. It may or may not be possible to discern the anguish disguised by such alarming behaviour.

Such an individual will have become overexcited and overstressed in the face of exceptional demands, and too desperate and overwrought to face the underlying grief and pain and guilt and worry. It will probably unwittingly have seemed necessary to that person to suppress any expression of distress as much as possible, and to keep all the agony to himself. And the agony will be extreme.

Perhaps he or she may have been bought up to believe it wrong or dangerous to show feelings. "Little boys don't cry" can be ingrained in the personality. Or perhaps there has just been no sufficient opportunity, time or place to admit to the natural feelings and process them. Either way, the hidden distress of the person has not yet been met, and there has been no space to begin to make sense of it all.

So underlying anger, fear, frustration, rejection, and pain compound the excessive excitement, and contribute greatly to blowing everything out of proportion. Other people will be frightened by the power of all the emotion and energy.

Inner stresses may have become so extreme that the person may be living on the edge of fight or flight all the time, utterly restless, and desperately untrustworthy, without sleep, out of touch with true reality, exceptionally speedy and perpetually driven by adrenalin. Hypomania like this can get worse if help is not heeded.

If all hope is abandoned of ever being able to share what is truly on the heart with anyone else, desperation increases. But the anguish is totally denied. This situation is very frustrating for others because it seems that nothing can be done to stop the person, or to begin a sensible conversation. For the afflicted person, the pain is totally denied and therefore does not exist. For those with eyes to see, however, the agony is extreme.

Ideas become grandiose, feelings of love overwhelming, visions mystical. As the situation worsens the person may become grossly over-familiar, irresponsible and aggressive. Speech may flow so fast that no one can make sense of it. This is mania. It is a massive defence, in demonised power, against becoming vulnerable, breaking down and collapsing. I reckon the Gadarene madman who lived in the tombs (Mark 5, etc.) was probably manic like this.

Attitudes and demons may eventually be dealt with before God. But meanwhile, extreme measures and powerful drugs are usually essential these days. Sedation with drugs and incarceration in a safe place may become imperative. The person may become so dangerous that forcible restraint may be needed for safety. Physical methods of control and restraint need not be harmful. Weapons need not be used.

Let us remember, however, that Jesus met that Gadarene madman and healed him. And so, too, the presence of the Lord Jesus in one or more of his present day disciples can suddenly break the violence of mania and render the person open to the Lord's healing. First it may be necessary to take authority over the demons and bind them and pray the Lord's healing into that person's soul and body. But godly people can help the person out of it.

Dancing mania and other 'hysteria'

It is recorded that dancing mania broke out periodically in the Middle Ages, and its origin was similar. It followed the cataclysmic horrors of the Black Death, in which thousands died very suddenly and whole populations were wiped out in a few days.[41]

Harrowing experiences of survivors of overwhelming events sometimes lead to manic reactions, which can be infectious. Other people without a sufficiently substantial knowledge of God, and without sufficient godly understanding to process such devastating horror, may join the mania, in denial of terrifying, overwhelming, seemingly inexpressible, incomprehensible emotion.

It may be almost impossible to say anything at all for many years about the most appalling experiences. Cataclysmic events may be too much to speak of for a very long time, so a person may become morose and unsociable, and the person may totally refuse to approach areas of experience that could in any way remind them of what happened.

This sort of suppressed denial occurs when the hidden memory of the overwhelming stress and horror has chronically fatigued the body. For example, it is often only as they have approached the end of their lives that holocaust survivors have been able to speak about what they suffered.

As death comes closer it is often natural to recall previously hidden events of one's life - in order, perhaps, naturally to find as much peace as possible. However, there are people whom Jesus has healed of the effects of the most terrible trauma not very long after it happened, and their evidence makes it clear that Jesus heals the very worst that mankind and the devil can inflict.[42]

"Where there is no vision the people perish"
So says Proverbs 29:18 (KJV). And if you have eyes to see it, after the seemingly inexplicable horrors two world wars western culture has been in denial. We have been manically

---

[41] Hecker, J.F.C., trans. Babington, B.G., (1844) *The Epidemics of the Middle Ages*, London, Sydenham Society.
[42] See Gashumba, F. (2007) *Frida*, Lancaster, Sovereign World.

seeking technological quick fixes for the horrors that unredeemed human nature has proved capable of. Some people even deny the holocaust. And the 'Christian' world seems largely to have been unable to comprehend the appalling carnage and genocide. Little or no biblical explanation is given or accepted by the secular world. There is little awareness that Matthew 24 may be exceedingly relevant today. Many have concluded that there is no God. Biblical wisdom, once partially assimilated within society, has been increasingly jettisoned and replaced by secular scientific humanism.

For those with eyes to see, a process of denial by the institutional church of the signs of the times, and of the deceptions and accusations of Satan, can actually be traced from the compromises made as a result of severe persecution of Christians in the first centuries, through the many heresies and philosophical deceptions perpetrated in subsequent centuries in the name of Christianity, to the worldly influences that prevailed upon the church with the Renaissance of Greek learning. Theoretical rules and legalistic expectations killed compassion and empathy. The reality of the loving grace and healing presence of God, and the gift of his only begotten son Jesus, and his victory on the cross, has been lost to so many individual souls.

Monastery hospitals, during and after the Hundred Years War and the Black Death in Europe in the fourteenth century, were mostly inadequate. The Civil War in England, and the so-called Enlightenment, took humanism a stage further.[43] And now, after the two World Wars, unbelief may be reaching its apogee.

The institutional church has generally failed to provide adequate understanding of human suffering. There has been almost no one prophetically to address the devastation of persecutions, wars and terrors, to reveal God's love and purpose and his healing power. Only very few have ever humbled

---

[43] See Broadbent, E.H. (1931) *The Pilgrim Church*, Basingstoke, Pickering & Inglis Ltd., and my book *Engaging with Reality*.

themselves before God and asked him what he is doing and what has been going on and what we should do. There has been a dearth of awareness of the eschatological significance of events. Nevertheless, through his only begotten Son Jesus Christ God has always been speaking prophetic words and bringing a people out of it all for himself (1 Peter 2:9, etc.).

Where there is no godly understanding of what is and what has been going on, including the most terrible devastations, and where there is no revelation and no prophetic voice, the people cast off restraint and perish (Proverbs 29:18). This is one vital reason why true disciples of Jesus should not neglect meeting one another's extreme distresses in a godly way, and seeking God's face together, and offering God's healing to others in these end times.

Those people who do indeed have eyes to see, and to meet the pain and wretchedness and sorry state of other people, may sometimes, perhaps, allow themselves to become quite overburdened by it all. They may even find themselves overworking in order to do all the philanthropic good they can to try to make the world a better place, without realising that they may be running away from the grief of being able to do only so very little, and of seeming unable to tell other people about Jesus and about God's justice, so as to open their eyes to the salvation available to them, and have the relief of sharing the burden. What is going on can be desperately oppressive when you see it. It can sometimes make you depressed, if you let it, and if you fail to cast all your cares on Jesus as they come. It is all God's business, after all, and our tears and groans all belong inside his wineskin (Psalm 56:8, Romans 8:18-27).

So perhaps it may not be mistaken to be dejected or depressed sometimes. It may even be healthy, for God can use the agony of our burdens to reveal himself to us and change us to understand his ways better and be obedient. Jacob (Genesis 28-29 and 31-34), Joseph (Genesis 37-41) Moses (whose story is in Exodus), Elijah (1 Kings 19), Jeremiah (Jeremiah 20) and David, (Psalm 55), Daniel

(1:1-15), Ezekiel (Chapter 4, and 24:18) and Hosea (1:2) all went through times of very considerable suffering, probably with periods of despair.[44] There are some people like Job, too, free of specific sin, free of specific wounds, free of wrong soul ties, and free of demons, whom God nevertheless allows to be severely oppressed by adversity ('depressed' in modern parlance) in order to refine them like gold (Proverbs 17:3; Hebrews 11:32-38), so that they shall see God and give a better account both here and hereafter.

The Lord Jesus himself was equipped and made perfect through suffering (Hebrews 2:10 and 5:7-10).

---

[44] Wilkerson, D. *An Eclipse of Faith*, 'Sword' magazine, Volume 3 No. 4 (July/August 2008).

7

HYSTERIA AND PERSONALITY DISORDER

Shut-down

Neuroimaging techniques can show parts of the brain shutting down and other parts opening up as a consequence of the sensory and motor activity of the body and of what is going on in the mind. But the mind is not the brain. The mind belongs to "the ghost in the machine". The mind is concerned with living relationships.

Although the mind is spiritual, its activity is regulated by connections in the physical body, most notably by physiological sensory mechanisms and memory. For those who are spiritually aware, what a person understands at any given time is determined not only through experience, perceived in context using memory recorded physiologically in the body, but also through spiritual revelation that comes through living relationships. I believe this includes relationships with spiritual beings who have no physical form, by whom we are always culturally influenced whether we know it or not.

Thus we respond to experience by interpretation which may actually be physiologically limited, controlled and censored. What is acted upon and what comes into personal awareness is influenced by reasoning that is limited by past understanding and spiritual allegiance. And although neuroimaging techniques may illustrate the physiology of the censoring activity, they cannot demonstrate what relevant material, from memory and from the mind, may be being shut out of consciousness.[45] And although they may demonstrate brain activity, they do not portray the mind.

Nevertheless, neuroimaging techniques do serve to demonstrate how parts of the brain can shut down outside of conscious control. Shut-down or inhibition of parts of the brain may sometimes occur in order to protect the person from being overwhelmed, whether by excessive, traumatic or confusing experience, reactivation of unhealed memory, or by powerful spiritual influence.

The living spirit of a person is constrained into living in a body in this world and thereby becomes subjected to worldly experience. The human spirit is fatally subject to corruption until a person is born again of the Holy Spirit (Romans 7:5), who enables us to overcome in obedience to God. When a person accepts Jesus and is baptised in Holy Spirit, that person becomes a new creation (2 Corinthians 5:17, Romans 6:4). What follows this new birth is a process that takes time and involves healing as the Holy Spirit tends to open up every aspect of the person, breaking through inhibitions and defences when the time is right and changing, healing and sanctifying the person (Romans 5:3-5, Romans 8:13, Ephesians 5:14).

Thus the Holy Spirit affects the living physiology, which therefore logically must be considered part of the soul. Eventually the whole person, spirit, soul and body can become transformed and perfected (1 Thessalonians 5:23-24). But until such healing has taken place, the Holy Spirit can be reflected in the life of a person only imperfectly. The word of God is that we are to make every effort to be holy (Hebrews 12:14). And this begins with

---

[45] Please refer to Chapters 1 to 4 of my book *Healing for the Wounded Life* for fuller discussion of the nature of mind and the inter-relationship of spirit, soul, physiology and body, and also of how concepts and language used in Christian healing may need to differ from those used by non-believers and secular science.

accepting in your heart what Jesus did for you on the cross, and following him.

Until God's healing is found for our past experience, the mechanisms that open up and shut down the activity in the brain will not be operating in the full peace of God, and therefore will be associated with some degree of stress. The chronic stress of always automatically controlling such split off, unhealed memory may eventually, after many years, become a cause of depression or other illness.

Dissociation from unhealed past experience

Certain experiences can cause parts of the brain to be shut down that otherwise would not be shut down if the person were healed through Jesus. The shut-down can affect thoughts and feelings and behaviour. Thus the expression of the person's spirit, through the personality, becomes limited by unhealed physiological censorship activity protecting the soul from being overwhelmed.

In this way conditions develop that are these days called *hysteria* and personality disorder. However, the Bible describes them in terms of a person's spirit being faint (Psalm 143:3-4) or broken (Job 17:1) or crushed (Psalm 34:18, Proverbs 17:22). And Psalm 34:18, Psalm116, Isaiah 61:1 and Luke 4:18 make it clear that God will heal this sort of thing.

Medical diagnosis was not such a big issue in Old Testament days, nor was the expectation of technological treatment. What everyday language then described as commonplace conditions of the human soul is now commonly reckoned to be illness. Nowadays we tend to ignore how the state of the soul may affect both personal behaviour and the physical body, but this was not the case for Hebrew contemporaries of Jesus.

The shutting down of parts of the brain that can be demonstrated on neuroimaging screens has not been correlated with what has been described in an earlier chapter as the censor. Trouble in the soul and loss of specific memories (as distinguished from loss of a function of the body) do not correlate with neuroimaging records. A so-called 'hysterical' loss of use of a limb will, however, show up on neuroimaging. But what may be going on in the mind and memory in connection with this loss of function will not. It is only when memory is eventually recovered and begins to be allowed into conscious awareness that such loss of function can begin to be correlated with material that has not been healed.

We must conclude that if a traumatic, unhealed memory of an event threatens to be remembered there may be some sort of protective inhibition and shut down of any function that threatens to facilitate the full memory. Thus either bodily function or behaviour, or both, can be affected. It is as though a fuse blows so that the relevant parts of the body will not remember, since full recall might dangerously and overwhelmingly threaten the functional integrity of the whole person in the present circumstances.

If full recall of any memory, or full consciousness of any current experience, threatens seriously to overwhelm the soul, the experience will be stored and kept in an inaccessible fashion, and behaviour will be adjusted effectively to displace the person from the full impact of the reality. The full memory will stay hidden until such a time as it either seems safe or advantageous for it to come to light. Histrionics of one sort or another are therefore always produced by the unspeakable.

The presence of the Holy Spirit amongst non-judgemental people, however, can make truthful recall safe, and healing possible. When the moment is right the presence of the Lord will enable recall of events that have hitherto been unmentionable. Then there may be some catharsis and repentance. The soul is healed as sins, wounds, spiritual bondages and unclean spirits are revealed and dealt with in the presence of God in the name of Jesus. The healing will beget a freeing of the personality. Godly character can then be built, with growth in maturity and wisdom. As healing progresses, the person may spontaneously say that their spirit now feels free, no longer faint or broken or crushed. As the soul is healed, the personality changes to reflect the new life of the Holy Spirit.

Manifestations of unhealed memory

Behaviour that signals the hidden presence of unhealed memory is like never letting your left hand know what your right hand is doing; or never letting your mother know the crime you committed; or being unable to think about the car accident in which your friend was killed but you, the driver, survived; or being so very frightened of censure and rejection that you remain unable to speak about what something utterly momentous did to you; or being too frightened of being subjected to further torture to speak the truth; or having been exposed to extreme emotions that are still so confusing that it seems impossible to understand them; or still being so shocked and frightened of falling apart and going mad that it remains impossible to open up a certain area of your life; or seeming to have markedly different personalities in different situations.

All these, and similar oddities, indicate that there may be aspects of memory and personality effectively too dangerous to be revealed. There is a splitting off, inhibition and shut down of anything that threatens to remind you of an unhealed aspect of yourself.

Often this will have originated in some sort of trauma, or serious accusation, or agonising deception so painful that it is not generally available to consciousness. This so-called dissociation is not wilful; rather it is an act of the automatic censor described in Chapter 2. It is an automatic inhibition that in a particular time and place protects the mind of the individual from being overwhelmed by remembered events.[46] It can result in various

---

[46] Mollon, P. (1998) *Remembering Trauma*, Chichester. John Wiley & Sons. Also McNally, R.J. *Remembering Trauma*, Harvard University Press.

forms of odd behaviour which can sometimes be associated with neurological shut-down detectable by neuroimaging techniques.

Out of body experiences

Mention was made in Chapter Three (on Trance) about experiments that had artificially produced out-of-body experiences, which are another manifestation of dissociation and so-called splitting or fragmentation of the personality, in which the person seems transported elsewhere although the body remains where it is. It seems from such experiments that the mechanism of dissociation occurs within the living body, involving both the soul and the physiology, so the actual manifestation is in the realm both of experience and behaviour. The person has the experience of being separated from the body, and those to whom he or she is well known may perhaps perceive him or her to be in some sort of trance. After first automatically dissociating at a time of acute trauma and confusion, which will have been produced by fearful shock, sometimes even in some sort of torture or ritual, a person may sometimes learn to dissociate in this way again at will.[47] Such a person may interpret their experiences spiritually and have apparently accurate revelations of travelling long distances and engaging in relationships in the spirit which affect other people. This is called astral travel.[48] The spiritual revelation is usually demonic.

The person can be set free through the healing of the initial trauma through which dissociation was first learned, and reconciling all experience to God. Associated demons will have to be expelled in the name of Jesus. But recall of original shock and trauma and subsequent events can be excessively disturbing unless true healing in the presence of the Lord Jesus is available.

---

[47] Sinason, V. (Ed.) (1994) *Treating Survivors of Satanist Abuse*, London, Routledge.
[48] Prince, D. and R. (1990) *Prayers and Proclamations*, Baldock, Derek Prince Ministries, contains handy material for self-protection.

Hysteria

Subconscious or unconscious memory is stored in the physical body as well in hidden recesses of the human spirit. In order to keep full memory from being accessible, behaviour has to be adjusted to control the parts of the body and personality that were involved with it. If the full import of the experience were actually to be remembered the experience might involve a re-living of the original trauma, which would be overwhelming.

This is how flashbacks happen.[49] Something in the pattern of current events triggers a memory, which is suppressed with difficulty, often with considerable torment. Strong drugs of one sort or another are often abused unwisely to try to kill the pain of the experience. Holy Spirit and the presence of the Lord will do it much better.

If extreme circumstances should again overcome a person who learned in childhood to dissociate automatically, and to split off their consciousness from experiences that threatened to be overwhelming, the event may prove so traumatic as to cause the alteration of a physiological function. As mentioned above, this sort of condition is traditionally given the medical label <u>hysteria</u>.

The function lost usually bears some simple logical connection not only to the recent trauma but also to the initial trauma as well. Memory of trauma sustained long ago in childhood - commonly before the age of eight – will have been triggered by recent events. It will have threatened to overwhelm the person and will have been suppressed, with consequent functional loss.

Thus to some extent the actual distress both of the recent traumatic experience and the past traumatic experience can be expressed through the odd symptoms, without the risk of becoming overwrought by total recall.

Thus, for example, the voice may be lost in the heat of the moment when what needs to be said cannot be said by a person

---

[49] Flashbacks are intrusive experiences of reliving previous trauma.

who, as a child, was disbelieved when she told her priest about incest with her father. Or the use of a limb may be lost, instead of using it to kill someone, by a person who has always carried guilt about having hit a baby brother just before he died. And excessive shocks and stress of battle may produce loss of various bodily functions in soldiers for similar reasons (which, after all, are fairly common). Globus hystericus (inability to swallow) may be produced by not being able to swallow something, either physical or metaphorical, in a person who is repressing a hidden memory of having almost suffocated when forced to swallow their vomit as punishment when a child. Hysterical blindness may be produced after shocking sights reactivate intolerable memory of events witnessed in childhood. The function of memory may be lost in this sort of way, too, in a person subconsciously reminded of repressed guilt and self-condemnation.

All sorts of various cramps, tremors, losses of sensation, speech difficulties, strange sensations in the genitals or in the stomach, and so on, may occur to prevent ancient and intolerable memories from coming into consciousness. Pseudo-pregnancy may develop when getting pregnant with the person you are in love with seems impossible but that person is reawakening hidden longings from a sexual relationship in childhood. Sleepwalking helps a soul to accommodate to disturbing events in recent daily life that threaten to reactivate unspeakable old memories. Likewise a person may sometimes wander off somewhere in a state of fugue, escaping from some reawakened traumatic memory that circumstances have triggered, without consciously intending to do so, or knowing why. Or a person may adopt very different personality characteristics originally assumed to disguise overwhelming childhood events.

Healing
Given time to adjust to what has recently occurred, 'hysterical' symptoms will often disappear. However such symptoms always

144

indicate that there is unhealed, hidden memory of previous trauma within the soul. The recent trauma, which caused a hysterical reaction to be manifest, will have reactivated old unconscious unhealed memory. Both the recent trauma and the past trauma will need the Lord's healing.

It must be emphasised that the person will not be consciously aware of the unhealed, hidden memory, not even when suffering hysterical symptoms. Even during flashbacks memory is likely to be partial and distorted.

Truer facts only begin to emerge when the person has the leisure and inclination to get to the root of why recent traumatic stress should have caused such a profound reaction over which they have had no control. As the person is patiently helped to connect one thought with another (which may sometimes be accompanied by a great deal of resistance to remembering), the process will lead to hidden memory of trauma.

If the original trauma took place in early childhood, it could be sexual. Memories of such things were buried because they could not be accepted, told about or understood at the time. The emotional reaction seemed overwhelming, and may still threaten to be so.

Sometimes it is necessary to have the help of a psychotherapist gently to allow the person to admit the truth about the hidden wounds. If all the emotion is expressed too violently all at once the person could be re-traumatized, without real relief. The truth of what occurred, and the subsequent effects, should patiently be taken into God's presence for healing in the name of Jesus. The demons should be bound in Jesus' name and the wounds healed. Afterwards the demons of fear and rage, and so on, can be expelled.

Freud and psychoanalysis

Sigmund Freud's earliest studies in psychoanalysis involved people who consulted him with hysteria.[50] It was a more common condition in those days than it is today, because the matters we have been discussing are now spoken about more openly.

Several of his patients revealed sexual assaults in childhood. At first he believed that such accounts were true. It may be hard for us to realise, more than a century later, how courageous Freud was not only to listen to what lay behind a condition that most professionals dismissed as the invention of women with weak minds but also to publish what he found, connecting hysteria, with details of sexual abuse and incest.[51]

The opposition Freud faced was intense, even more intense than is the opposition to investigating the truth about the abduction and abuse of children today. It seems, too, that some of the opposition was anti-Semitic.

Within a few years, however, Freud had publicly repudiated his belief that such histories were true. He seems to have come to believe they were fantasies reinforced in childhood by masturbation. Then he was no longer so ostracised because he was no longer exposing the pagan sexuality and cruelty, of adults against children, which lay beneath the surface of European "Christian" respectability.

In consequence, he was able, with other respectable doctors, to develop the theory and practice of institutional psychoanalysis. I do personally wonder, however, if perhaps he may secretly have hoped that psychoanalysis would eventually lead to a full

---

[50] Freud, S. *The Aetiology of Hysteria*, a paper read before the Society for Psychiatry and Neurology, Vienna, April 21, 1896. James Strachey's translation of this paper may be found in Masson, J.M. (1984) *The Assault on Truth*, published by Fontana in 1992.

[51] When he read his academic paper he may not, perhaps, have realised how incredulous fellow intellectuals would be.

exposure of the truth – which has, in fact, indirectly been the case. But there is no actual evidence that this occurred to him.

The massively influential body of psychoanalytic theory that has subsequently been built up is essentially a scheme for connecting unconscious fantasy, (spelled 'phantasy' by psychoanalysts proudly to protect their intellectual monopoly) with conscious mental activity and behaviour. But psychoanalysis has been a considerable blessing to mankind because it has involved careful listening, to the relief of many people who longed seriously to be heard.

Orthodox psychoanalytic theory is humanistic and denies that we are created in the image of God (Genesis 1:27). It denies the hard reality of evil and sin - for they cannot truly be accommodated without Messiah Jesus. It avoids any notion that our development from childhood to adulthood can be powerfully affected by godly or ungodly spiritual influences. It considers human nature in its fallen state without recognising it as fallen. It has a Hebrew understanding and compassion for human nature but it applies a sophisticated lex talionis, explaining consequences but unable to offer real healing.

To a Christian with living faith in Jesus it seems mistaken to speak of our progressive development and its vicissitudes in terms of symbol and fantasy, and unnecessary to invent special terms when godly reality can be addressed in ordinary language. Evidence uncovered through psychoanalysis, however, is worthy of serious study even if conclusions have been misconstrued by classical psychoanalytic theory.

Freud came from a fairly prosperous Jewish family, and seems to have kept some Jewish traditions. But he rebelled against the faith. Significantly he ignored and refuted the God of the Tanakh of his people, and his understanding of man and woman and relationships denied the power and influence of deities although, interestingly, he accumulated a vast collection of idols. Sadly, his vision was limited by his worries about earning a respectable living, his spiritual rebellion and unbelief, and his classical Greek humanism. His interest in people was warm and sensitive, nevertheless. In contrast to many other psychologists, he did not apply scientific measurement, but rather endeavoured to engage with people directly to help them discover what he believed to be an adequate understanding for what they were experiencing. But he invented a system of humanistic reasoning to explain what he observed without including God.

He should have known from Torah what the nations who worship other gods are really like (see Leviticus 18:24). If he had read the word of God in the light of the Holy Spirit he would not have misconstrued the truth his patients were trying to tell him. He would not have rooted his "Oedipus complex" so firmly in his invented theory of childhood sexuality.[52] He would have known Father God could heal the trauma and confusion and helplessness and fear and shame and guilt of a sexually abused child (read Jeremiah 31).And he would have known that same Father God, the creator of the universe, would give him the strength to stand up for the truth in the face of truth-haters (Psalm 72:12-14, Proverbs 31:8-9).

What the psychoanalysts with their limited understanding have called the life instinct, or libido, should be known to be the breath of life given to everybody from God, and what the psychoanalysts have called the death instinct should be known to be the curse of the fall from grace (Genesis 2:17 and 3:22-24).

By avoiding the politics, legal controversies and social action that could have stolen his time had he persisted in declaring publicly that he believed his patients, however, he was able not only to remain active as a physician and ameliorate his patients' distress, but also to contribute significantly to the understanding of human nature. Most people would accept that the experiences of childhood shape the course of life, and Freud drew attention to

---

[52] The Greek myth of Oedipus is important. My Christian interpretation of it is given in Chapter 7 (page 138) of *Healing for the Wounded Life*, and my discussion of childhood sexuality is in Chapter 6 of that book.

this. He also made it respectable to speak about the profound significance of personal experience, and he wrote engagingly about deep issues people recognised. They say Freud was a loving man; and he once described psychoanalysis as a treatment that works through love.[53] And he kept faith with people as best he could. And even when his conclusions were wrong they were useful.

The battle for truth is spiritual, and Freud was only partially equipped. Weapons that are powerful enough are only given to disciples of the Lord Jesus.[54]

The very worst of human nature

There is no reason for any true Christian to suppose that any horror, or any torture, or any pagan ritual that has ever occurred to mankind, has not been inflicted by human beings on other human beings or by adults on children – sometimes even in the name of Christianity (although never truly in the name of the Lord Jesus Christ of Nazareth). Such events mostly happen out of sight, and they only rarely result in criminal trials.

Many of those who have been extensively involved with the deep issues of the minds and hearts and souls and bodies of people in prisons and psychiatric units know the truth of what people do, but they mostly keep quiet about it, both for want of adequately corroborative evidence and also because it disturbs people too much. Evil has enormous secret power in many people's lives, in all cultures. Satan is brilliantly clever, but the Lord Jesus Christ of Nazareth overcame Satan and won a permanent victory over him when he died on the cross and rose

---

[53] *The Freud/Jung Letters,* tr. Mannheim and Hull, 1974: letter from Freud to Jung dated 6 December 1906.
[54] Only through Jesus can Satan be overcome, truth be fully revealed and the wounds fully healed. Sadly, neither Masson, J. (1984) in *The Assault on Truth – Freud and Child Sexual Abuse,* published by Fontana in 1992, nor Miller, A. (1981) in *Thou Shalt Not Be Aware – Society's Betrayal of the Child,* London, Pluto Press 1985, knew this.

from the dead on the third day. Jesus now sits at the right hand of God to intercede for those who call on him to be saved (Hebrews 7:25). And God gives authority to overcome with incomparably great power to those who make Jesus their saviour, and accept him as their redeemer because his blood was shed to make atonement for them (Ephesians 1:5-7 and 19-23). People who do not really know Jesus like this must, to a large extent, stay blind to evil, because to open their eyes and ears to it could be overwhelming (John 9:39).

Aspects of life commonly ignored by Christianity

Psychoanalysis has attempted to study the roots of distress, and it is a blessing that it has made it fashionable in some quarters to assume responsibility for oneself through bringing issues to light in a sort of confession, and subjecting them to 'analysis'. The student needs to be discerning enough, and self-controlled enough, to see the relevance of the partial truths of psychoanalysis. Despite its deficiencies, and despite the defensiveness and exclusiveness of psychoanalytic institutions, the nature of mental illness may then begin to unfold.

Psychoanalysis is influenced both by Judaism and by humanism and, although it does not acknowledge sin, it has yielded valuable insights through bringing to light aspects of the human soul long ignored by Christianity, in particular the difficulties of adhering to moral law through powers of natural reason. It has therefore been an effective weapon against the forces that would dehumanise people and use them as pawns.

Perhaps God allowed that Jewish physician to develop psychoanalysis in order to enable psychotherapists, and even a few Christian priests and healers, to be credited with sufficient respectability to be allowed to listen to people and take them seriously for as long as it may take for healing to be found.

Group healing work

Two World Wars eventually convinced a minority of psychiatrists, all of them to some extent working within the Judeo-Christian tradition, that trauma (physical or psychological) could affect a person's mind and behaviour, and that to be wounded in this way was not malingering. In consequence fewer soldiers were executed for cowardice or desertion.

Some traumatized combatants were able to benefit from telling their appalling experiences to each other in groups, and seriously listening to each other in the same way that psychotherapists listen.[55] Often there was distress. But the environment held together and contained it, and so was safe. So there was relief, and healing.

Even the more distant memories of childhood trauma are more easily remembered in such an environment. Amongst others who have had similar experiences, sense can be made of what previously could not be articulated.

It came to be accepted amongst some members of the psychiatric profession that sharing with others, all of whom know from their own personal experience a lot about what is being related, is an effective means of healing neuroses and disorders of personality caused by overwhelming trauma. A respected referee who has sufficient understanding, and sufficient wisdom to allow light to penetrate deception and darkness, proves to be essential - otherwise the material will not effectively be contained.

It was found necessary to make the milieu for such group-work safe enough by creating a body of theory credible enough for authorities to pay for the necessary environment to be made available. Regrettably, however, since much of such theory has not only been resistant to quantitative scientific measurement but also open to various interpretations, according to differing belief systems, secular administrative authorities have subsequently felt

---

[55] This was notably put into practice at the Northfield Military Hospital in the U.K. during the Second World War.

uncertain of what they would be paying for. Nor have they had the vision to provide proper facilities.

Because people are vulnerable to manipulation when they lower their protective personal defences, it is necessary to account credibly for the system of belief and thought under which such facilities operate. So this sort of treatment has fallen out of favour because secular humanistic multifaith politics have not found reason enough to believe in it.

Possibilities for group work in churches

Perhaps, for those who would turn to Jesus, it could become the business of churches, instead of secular welfare agencies, to provide the necessary environment. The number of people suffering secretly from the effects of trauma of one sort or another is enormous and this work would build faith and revive churches through applying the word of God to common experience without making secular humanistic judgements.

Healing unemployment and criminality

Soon after the Second World War more people began to realise, from the evidence of the damage that war could inflict on the mind, that not only inability to hold down a job, but also criminal behaviour, might be caused by distressing and traumatic past experience. People with poor employment records, began to be rehabilitated through group therapy.[56] British prisons made psychotherapeutic rehabilitation available, involving detailed personal accountability both to an intimate group and to the larger therapeutic community under careful supervision, for

---

[56] Notably at the Social Rehabilitation Unit at Sutton, Surrey, UK, which subsequently became a therapeutic community called The Henderson Hospital for people with personality disorders, recently closed by the National Health Service. See Rapoport, R.N.(1960) *Community as Doctor*, London, Tavistock Publications (1959) Ltd.

volunteers serving long sentences who were genuinely seeking in-depth change and healing.[57]

Possibilities of group work for psychiatric conditions

Later a few scattered psychiatrists began to realise how mental illness could develop as a result of past distress and trauma, including the trauma of distorted relationships. Similar group and community therapy was attempted in one or two psychiatric hospitals with good results.[58] Although this is no longer accepted practice, it is still successfully used in modified form for the treatment of addiction.[59]

Inadequacy of secular methods

The search for healing for psychological trauma, however, has rather given way to liberal intellectual and academic exploration of what may be going on in interpersonal relationships. This has opened the field for suspension of judgement, and for the influx of all sorts of beliefs and theories, many of them far from the Judeo-Christian ideal.

It became apparent that some degree of ease of stress could be found simply by exploring, and then justifying and accrediting, all sorts of diverse attitudes and behaviours.[60]

---

[57] This first started at Wormwood Scrubs Prison in London in 1946. Grendon Prison opened in 1962 and has been totally devoted to this work. See Gunn, J., Robertson, G., Dell, S., and Way, C. (1978) *Psychiatric Aspects of Imprisonment*, London, Academic Press, also Genders, E. and Player, E. (1995) *Grendon – A Study of a Therapeutic Prison*, Oxford, Clarendon Press.

[58] Shenley Hospital and Claybury Hospital in north London were examples. See Martin, D.V. (1962) *Adventure in Psychiatry, Social Change in a Mental Hospital*, Oxford, Bruno Cassirer. See also Main, T. (1946) *The Hospital as a Therapeutic Institution*, Bulletin of the Meninger Clinic 10, p.66.

[59] Notably in Alcoholics Anonymous, but also in many private rehabilitation units.

[60] Main, T. (*op. cit.*) with his "culture of enquiry" and Sullivan, H.S., with his theme that psychiatric conditions are essentially problems of interpersonal relationships (see his *Interpersonal Theory of Psychiatry*, 1953, London, Tavistock Publications Ltd.) powerfully influenced this humanistic trend.

Nevertheless, speaking openly, in an accepting group (amongst peers who understand but brook no nonsense, and manage effectively to contain the narratives and the emotion), about issues that have caused distress and affected one's adaptability and behaviour, is a most efficient way for traumatized and distressing people to begin to find healing.[61] In this sort of milieu a Christian may fairly efficiently discover what needs to be brought to God in the name of Jesus for healing of the root causes (James 5:16).

Personality disorder

Most people said to have a personality disorder are those who have habitually caused social disruption and inflicted many personal wounds on others one way or another. Their behaviour will usually have been intractably disturbing from early childhood. Those with eyes to see can understand how it originates in fear, anxiety, worry, trauma, abuse, confusion, neglect, injustice, and violence from the adults amongst whom the person has grown up. They can also understand that this will be denied, and will not become fully apparent through formal history taking.

Within the child's family and culture there would have been no effective knowledge of divine forgiveness, no faith in God or real knowledge of his love and truth and justice. There would therefore have been no sound basis for the healing of wounds of the soul. Deities who are not benign may have been worshipped.

From earliest childhood the person will have reacted to events in keeping with their fallen human nature, or worse. Bad events will have produced habitual bad reactions, wreaking much havoc and destruction. There will be many old wounds in the soul that

---

61 Serious personal distress and mental illness is tackled in this way both at the Arbours Crisis Centre and also within the Philadelphia Association, both in London., and in other secular organisations. Neither the state nor insurance companies, however, will these days pay for the time this sort of healing takes.

154

will have produced complex patterns of reactive sin. Social conscience will be limited to expedient loyalty to the rebellious subculture of family, gang or clan. The person will be demonised, liable to sudden extremes of disturbing behaviour, and adept at deception. And quite frequently deception may take the form of a sophisticated veneer of social respectability with a brilliant facility for lying. Many such chronically antisocial or criminal people end up in prison.[62]

The trauma of incest or sexual or ritual abuse, beginning when a child is too young to recognise the violation, may not be felt until the effects begin to be felt much later when the person is old enough to come into sufficient contact with other people to begin to be more aware of what happened.

The abuse may have led to precocious sexuality with lasting repercussions, including pregnancies, promiscuity, bitterness of soul, self-hatred, suicide attempts, thieving, violence, and all sorts of other trouble, and many other people may have been distressed in consequence. Or it may have led to chronic confusion, fears, self-harm, forgetfulness, lack of spontaneity and a dreadfully crushed spirit. As the effects become apparent there may be many flashbacks, and much shame, rage, confusion, conflict, and hopelessness. A person may become apathetic and say they are all in pieces and some may describe their personality as fragmented. Other people may become seductive and biddable, as though they are unable to be discerning or have a will of their own to say "No!" when appropriate.[63] Many become addicted to drugs.

---

[62] Prison could be the best place for such people to find help because many of them need to be behind bars for it to be safe for them to receive it. Many prisons need the vision for this.

[63] People can become like this when the trauma has been so prolonged that they have been given up hope. All their cries for help came to nothing and no one believed them.

Serious trauma occurring later in life may also produce disorders of personality. Catastrophic events, war, accidents, torture are profoundly shocking. The shock, fear and wounds may remain buried in the soul. The person will automatically censor any reminder. Unclean spirits of fear, rage, violence, murder, unforgiveness, retaliation, and so forth, are often attached to those hidden wounds of the soul and may suddenly manifest themselves through the personality if they are triggered. Healing takes time and several strong men may sometimes be needed if there is much resistance to repentance.

All our infirmities may be laid on Jesus. Because of the wounds Jesus suffered we may really receive comfort and healing from God (Isaiah 53:4-5) and be delivered. The punishment that brings us peace was upon Jesus. The presence of God with us, his Holy Spirit, heals. We thank God for his only begotten Son and for his wonderful grace.

Personality traits

If wounding of the soul has not been quite so severe or prolonged, personality traits may be automatically adopted that not only help to keep the wounds hidden but that are also just about tolerable to other people, traits such as chronic aloofness, chronic obsessionality, chronic paranoia, or even periodic histrionics. Many people with difficult traits of personality find a niche in society and are more or less accepted by others with good humour as eccentrics. Nevertheless, their wounds may be deep, and God by his grace will heal such chronically ungodly attitudes in Jesus' name at the appropriate time and place.

Understanding trauma to the soul

If something terrible happens such as, for example, an accident in which someone dearly loved dies but you survive, after the initial shock and terrible distress some understanding eventually begins to be gained, and some peace begins to come if emotion can be expressed with sympathetic people and events are brought before God for his healing. The good example of others helps.

But if everyone is too shocked, or if people should pretend that what has happened has not happened, or if people disbelieve what you are feeling and deny the true significance of what has happened, or dismiss your distress and cannot understand you because of their own fears, any attempt to make sense of what happened may naturally begin to seem hopeless. In this case the memory of the trauma may be locked away, split off with all the emotion and confusion, and dissociated as much as possible from everyday affairs so as to keep life as normal as possible.

Any attempts to remember, furthermore, may be distorted by faulty understanding, confusing emotion, immature imagination and demons that have taken advantage of the situation. Flashback memories, full of this sort of torment, may sometimes occur out of the blue and be terrifying. So behaviour may be modified to prevent recall, and the person may consequently seem difficult or strange sometimes.

The full discharge of all the emotion connected with serious trauma could be so overwhelming as to re-traumatize the person, although this may be prevented if other genuine people are present who understand well enough to make the person feel safe enough. And when such people turn to Jesus for healing, churches should never fail to meet them in sincerity and truth (Luke 7:41-43) with compassion and hospitality. The effects of trauma may be disabling until the person can find safe people with whom to meet Jesus.

As previously described, locked-away memory can activate the censor to stop any future experience from fully reminding the person of the past trauma. In consequence, certain experiences are avoided or incompletely understood. At the same time, the locked away memory constantly causes some degree of stress to the person and may cause a fascination with circumstances, or with substances, that seem to ease the stress.

157

Locked away memory may also cause the person quite unconsciously to reconstruct circumstances similar to the original trauma, for example by getting into relationships similar to the relationships at the time of the hidden trauma, without realising the fact. This unconscious inner compulsion to repeat events connected to the trauma makes me believe that there is naturally an unconscious hope that one day healing may be found through re-living what happened.[64]

The consequence of such neurotic activity of the censor (this sort of activity can rightly be termed 'neurosis,' an affliction of the nerves) is that it may seem that part of the personality is immature, or that the development of part of the personality has been disordered (hence the term 'personality disorder'). Sometimes the person has come to believe that a there is a child inside them that is separate from the adult. And sometimes the person may hear voices that may or may not seem to belong to the person.

Sometimes, when traumata in childhood have been multiple and extensive, the person may believe their self to have several different personalities. The person has learned to behave differently in different circumstances so that the personality seems fragmented so as to keep safe from remembering and reactivating hidden trauma and distress. It may seem that there are several quite markedly different personalities within the same person, with differing sets of interests and abilities and emotional expressions and these different personalities may sometimes even have been given different names. If this becomes particularly obvious it is sometimes called <u>multiple personality</u>. This term is disliked by many professionals, however, because it tends to reinforce the dissociated state and make reintegration harder.

In the course of everyday life, situations will inevitably arise that threaten to remind the person with so-called personality

---

[64] See the section on Compulsive Repetition in Chapter 7 of *Healing for the Wounded Life*.

disorder of split off, inhibited, repressed experience. Such triggers may cause the person to panic without knowing why. Or they may trigger flashback memories of horror that cannot be understood. Or behaviour may become excessively exuberant in some way that seems to get rid of some of the repressed distress and emotion without the original trauma being consciously remembered, and such behaviour may become habitual. Other people usually find such a person very hard to cope with and those close to the person may require generous support over long periods of time.

The process of healing

God wants to heal every person from all that has happened in the past and from all associated deceptions and demons. So it is best to turn to the Lord Jesus Christ, the only begotten Son of God, confess your sin and bad behaviour, in detail, and give your life to him, and receive his forgiveness for real, and then listen to the Holy Spirit who will come to you. As time goes by the Holy Spirit will then make you aware of one thing after another to be put right with God for your healing. God may use his kingdom people to help with this. Truth will dawn and the pieces of the jigsaw of what you have experienced will come together. For your own sake be willing to forgive, because not to do so keeps you unrelentingly bitter, and may make you ill!

It can take time for falsehood to be separated from truth and for false guilt to become apparent and true guilt to be dealt with. The Lord will reveal truth as you can digest it, and when you are ready for it. The necessary truth will come out, despite all previous deception, provided the Holy Spirit is not stopped from doing his work. He knows it all anyway, but he will never make you deal with more than you can take (1 Corinthians 10:13). Since this is a process, it is necessary to be patient and to persevere if old habits seem to die hard.

The shock and trauma will need to be separated from the demons in the name of Jesus, and then healed by the Lord with prayer. Then any demons will need to be expelled in Jesus' name. The Lord may be asked to bring the personality together and to heal the brokenness, and the memories, and make relationships right.

Attending regular meetings with other people who understand or, better still, living in community can make the healing of such disorders of personality much easier. Community living is a good idea because people who are difficult to live with can overtax smaller groups and families. Other people who have suffered in a similar way, and other people you feel at home with and get to know fairly intimately, can ease the passage through what you may have to go through.

The word of God is necessary for guidance, with teaching relevant to raw experience, so that an adequate framework of understanding may be generated. Generosity, compassion and love of one's neighbour help to dissolve walls of splitting and dissociation so that fragments of the true person you are may come together. A culture of confession, repentance and healing, and of holding faithfully to the word of God in the presence of Jesus, makes it safe.

In this sort of environment memory may occasionally transport the whole person, body and soul, back to the time and place of earliest trauma, and behaviour may regress, which gives the illusion of being in the last place of safety ever really known before tragedy happened. With a fear of imminent disaster, it is as if it is all happening again now. So the person may automatically behave as a child and become strangely dependent on those who are being trusted. This is a way of remembering with the whole of one's being. If it is allowed to evolve, and if memories are sensibly met as memories, with the Lord's healing as appropriate, and not impeded, the person may find wholeness. It may be tempting to offer corrective experience, to give comfort where there was no comfort, and so on, but this does not assist permanent healing. God heals the facts of what happened.

There may be a great deal of emotion and confusion as trauma and deception are remembered. Catharsis in the presence of God is usually necessary to some extent, but if it is prolonged the person may be re-traumatized by the overwhelming emotion. It will be necessary to bind demons in Jesus' name whilst God begins the healing.

Transference

Furthermore, when people trust one another enough to speak openly together, without being defensive about things that may be embarrassing in more formal company, they often, by chance as it were, come to see some of the other people they are speaking with in a familiar way. This person seems like a brother, that person like mother, and so on. Then when they find themselves thinking and feeling about those people, and behaving towards them, in ways that in truth bear little connection with present reality, it may be seen that unconscious memory is influencing their thoughts and feelings and behaviour towards certain people.

Unconscious memory will have been activated by the similarity of an event, or the similarity of a person, to a significant event or person in the past; and this can be brought out into the light and spoken about to the benefit of everyone concerned. Healing comes from accepting that thoughts, feelings, attitudes and behaviour may be determined by unhealed events in the past as well as by present circumstances, and asking Father God to reveal truth and to break wrong attachments and to heal in Jesus' name.

Thus, for example, the way a man expressed impatience reminded a woman in the same group of her brother. To their mutual benefit he admitted to his current impatience, and found healing for it. But elements of her behaviour towards him, that had seemed to have nothing to do with him and had therefore excited his impatience, enabled that group of people to uncover details of the incestuous relationship that woman had had with

161

her brother in childhood, the memory of which had been automatically withheld because it had seemed too traumatic. So she was then able to receive the Lord's healing for the incest.

As described in Chapter 3 (on Trance) above, psychoanalysts and psychotherapists call this phenomenon, whereby unconscious memory is transferred into present circumstances, "transference". When this repressed material becomes conscious, and the person takes responsibility for it, there is said to be "insight". These are useful concepts.

Real healing can come when there is forgiveness and deliverance from wrong relationships in the name of Jesus. Amongst people who have come to know each other quite well, and have no axe to grind, you find that people will understand the thoughts, feelings and behaviour of others in this way quite readily.

Inadequacy of secular facilities

It can be a surprise to discover how many people suffer from seriously unhealed memories and how poorly hysteria and personality disorders are understood in health services by secular professionals. The reason for this is that secular services can only offer treatment that is free of Judeo-Christian bias, so that people of other faiths might not be offended.

Furthermore, only short-term treatment seems cost-effective to them, which in practice usually means suppression of symptoms with drugs, psychology and brief counselling.

When the fundamental spiritual roots of these distressing human conditions are not adequately addressed, a certain amount of distress will obviously continue. The healing that is needed is healing of the soul, through relationships with other people, under the authority of the Lord Jesus. The presence of the Lord brings the gift of repentance that enables the mind to let go of its strongholds and to change, so as to allow the presence and revelation of God to come in.

The healing comes essentially from God, through believing the Lord Jesus his only begotten Son, and with the help of the people he empowers for his work. So there is no point in leaving the healing of the minds and personalities of those who turn to Jesus to secular specialists. It is the business of the kingdom church.

Therefore every church group where there is any decent degree of freedom to come together into the name of Jesus in sincerity and truth, would actually be a healing group if the individuals in it were to be very tolerant of each other's weaknesses (1 Corinthians 8:9), and non-judgemental about sin that is being tackled. And they would do well to engage in healing talk and healing prayer with each other quite often, by way of applying gospel teaching, without imagining that they need specialist knowledge. This would build holiness. The Holy Spirit will tell them what to do.

"The tongue that brings healing is a tree of life..." (Proverbs 15:4) and "The Lord is close to the broken hearted and saves those who are crushed in spirit" (Psalm 34:18).

8

SCHIZOPHRENIA

Phenomenology and healing

Through no obvious fault of their own, people who have become schizophrenic may seem almost to have opted out of belonging amongst the human race. They seem to lack the individual soundness of mind that people expect of others. Unless the condition is controlled with drugs, common understanding may be lost and social norms to a greater or lesser extent may be ignored or mocked by them.

Whatever the person feels a need to communicate is often not plainly said. Unexpected meanings may be read into other people's behaviour. Communications may be received with apparent clarity from unusual sources, frequently from voices that other people do not hear.

What the schizophrenic person communicates through body language, mannerisms, postures, neologisms or strange juxtapositions of words and sentences may be puzzling or distressing to others, and may seem to conflict with the common sense, common meanings, common understandings, that most of us take for granted.

Relationships with other people seem to be guided by impulses and instincts that fail to give due heed to the sensitivities of others. The person has lost civilising influences, and reflects only solipsistically upon what he or she thinks or does. There is rejection, distrust, confusion, hopeless abandon to fate, an inner anxiety often disguised by prescribed drugs, and a strange impulsivity.

Inclusion in society very obviously becomes more tenuous. In fact the person seems to live in another world, and this can become so distressing for others that the afflicted person becomes effectively rejected and driven away from other people into institutional treatment because people quite naturally find it difficult to cope with having such a person around.

Human beings need sufficient truth in their complex relationships. Unlike the animals, we need a measure of willing and conscious accord with an essential security more profound than the culture we live in. When such accord is negated we lose our bearings and may quite easily give way to fickle caprice. Demonic influences can create interpersonal mis-takes that negate the truth on which individuals depend, driving people crazy.

The complex web of existential truth within the culture to which we look for everyday security is always being subjected to change. We people need an inner core of sufficient sound truth within us in order to adapt to changing circumstances.

There is a God of truth whose Spirit is known to mankind, who holds firm when everything in this world falls away. Psalm 95 describes him as the rock of our salvation. His salvation is known in practice to bring rest to the soul – see Psalm 62:1. Therefore we acknowledge that mankind was made in the image of God.

In this light a schizophrenic person may be regarded as having become resigned to an apparent absence of God's power and truth and saving grace. Behaviour may even appear so strange that people may perhaps be forgiven for sometimes likening it to that of animals, for whom the instincts of the herd must generally suffice. Animals do not have to think in any great depth about meaning, but human beings usually do.

In Chapter 4 of the Book of Daniel it is recorded that King Nebuchadnezzar of Babylon was "given the mind of an animal" for a time, after he had had a dream that had terrified him. Although the dream had been a divine challenge to his supreme power and authority, he would not subsequently acknowledge the hand of God and proudly persisted in setting himself above God. A year later, in consequence, he was "driven away from people" and lived "with the wild animals." I believe his loss of sanity would these days be called schizophrenia. And I believe is highly significant that his sanity was restored, and his authority returned to him, when he raised his eyes towards heaven and "praised the most high" and "glorified him who lives for ever." That is the way out of schizophrenia.

In Mark 1:13 we are told that Jesus also lived for a while with the wild animals in the desert, where he was tempted by Satan, although angels protected him. Furthermore, Jesus felt temporarily forsaken by God at the moment of his death on the cross (Matthew 27:46; Psalm 22:18). Because he has been in the place of the forsaken, we can be sure he knows about schizophrenia. And because God raised him from the dead we can be sure he will heal this condition if he is called upon to do so in the name of Jesus.

Double-mindedness

We human beings have freedom of will: the freedom either to hold to the ways and truths of our creator God who brings us peace or to discount them. When God is not honoured and glorified sufficiently in spirit and truth, either individually or collectively in the culture, and when the words and wisdom of God are ignored, we human beings lose God's light and truth from our society.

Then significant facts are misinterpreted, unpalatable facts remain hidden, law becomes increasingly unjust, compassion gives way to desperation, and people more commonly go mad (Matthew 5:14, Deuteronomy 28:28). And the madness is not understood, but treated with suppression of one sort or another.

When God's light and truth are confused or obscured, deadened through legalism, or effectively invalidated through dependency upon other spiritual powers, the way people's minds are made up lacks sufficient soundness to cope with major environmental change. Then people may not know which way to turn.[65] Instinct will be insufficient. Direction will not be affirmed through the Spirit of truth.

When people move away from a good relationship with God, and when nations cease to honour his dignified place amongst them, people move away from being able to receive his guidance and his blessing. God is just and true and is working out his purposes. He made us in his image, and his love for us is jealous. As people fall away from him there inevitably comes a time, therefore, when they become caught up in wrath and torment (Romans 1:16-19). Confusion, stultification and madness may result.

People may think they can ride out the torment. But they can't. Sooner or later they face the judgement of God.

Difficulties making sense of schizophrenia

I have never personally been schizophrenic but I have known and ministered to many people who have, and I have read around the subject and have gleaned extra understanding, by the grace of God, from published accounts of the experiences of people who passed through schizophrenia and recovered.[66]

Impediments to a general understanding of schizophrenia are inherent in the very nature of the condition. Ascertaining truth about the personal experience of schizophrenic people is difficult, for by the time they become overtly schizophrenic they have usually become used to disguising truth, and confused about

---

[65] In support of this assertion, note the anthropological work of Gregory Bateson which began with *Naven*, published in 1936 by Cambridge University Press. He demonstrated how schizogenesis may result from moving from the demands of one culture to the demands of another, and he developed the hypothesis that madness may arise from the consequent antinomy. However, because he did not personally acknowledge Jesus to be the light of the world he missed both the spiritual cause and the cure. Where paths meet, wisdom really does take her stand and call out for prudence, understanding, righteousness, truth and justice (Proverbs 8:2); but people fail to hear.

[66] Biographical accounts are listed in the Bibliography.

167

who and what is authentic, and their relationships have become so deceptive that the meaning of their language may be hard to decipher. They have often become incorrigibly alienated and many of them are out of circulation under institutional treatment.

Another common difficulty is a fear that by getting too close, and understanding too well, you could not only begin to uncover some very uncomfortable issues, that other people do not want revealed, but also that you could be accused of being mad yourself.[67]

Christians may, however, be reassured by the fact that Jesus himself was said to be mad (Mark 3:21, John 10:20), although there was, in truth, no madness in him at all, for he always obeyed his Father, the only wise God who heals. And Paul told how "God chose the lowly things of this world and the despised things – and the things that are not – to nullify the things that are" (1 Corinthians 1:28). Consequently I have persisted in using biographical material and in making judgments about madness with the Holy Spirit, rather than with academic psychiatry, as my guide (1 Corinthians 2:15).

When schizophrenic explanations seem facile and unintelligible, people stop trying to understand, and start instead to do something about the inconvenience the person seems to cause. Then what is believed and what is done frequently depend upon cultural prejudice. However, if someone with the Holy Spirit living in them is willing patiently to listen and, by the grace of God, to try to empathise, then the nature of schizophrenia may begin to unravel. Personally, I have often found it fairly easy to enjoy conversations with people deemed schizophrenic.

There is enormous cultural pressure in society not to contravene accepted mores, and to accept that accredited professionals will have considered all the relevant issues. Although Christian spiritual considerations are of supreme

---

[67] Note R D Laing and A Esterson, *Sanity, Madness and the Family,* London, Tavistock Publications, 1964.

significance they are most unlikely to have been taken into account these days. The perceived relevance of Christian spirituality to madness has been in decline for at least eight hundred years.

Theology has lost its supremacy amongst academic disciplines in consequence of compromises with fashionable humanistic thinking. Nowadays academic Christian theologians would probably lose their jobs if they were to realise how pertinent their discipline could be to the explanation of psychiatric phenomena, because they would be exposing issues that threaten everyday details of secular culture.

So now if someone schizophrenic does not receive the treatment deemed correct by the psychiatric establishment, there could be grounds for a lawsuit, in which the eventual judgement would probably fall in favour of established prejudices of culture and society rather than godly truth. Physicians who are younger than I am do not now have the freedom that I have had during my lifetime to earn their professional living relatively independently of the psychiatric establishment, which has increasingly come under state control. It is not so easy now for them to follow lines of enquiry that would inevitably lead to professional isolation, because they would be unable to earn a living. To make matters worse, anything not categorised as legal is increasingly liable to be deemed illegal, due to the encroachment of European law. And because most legislators are not Christian, biblical values are generally no longer understood. This pushes many Christian activities out of the mainstream into small, informal societies. Sadly it also encourages people to avoid unofficial involvement in the healing of people deemed mentally ill. Nevertheless, we shall here pursue a Christian understanding of madness for the sake of those who have the courage to turn to God for healing through his only begotten son Jesus.

Further empathetic conclusions

When listening to a lecture the other day my attention drifted away from the speaker and I became lost in my own train of thought for a while, and totally missed several sentences of what was said. For a few brief moments I lived in another world with my own reflections, memories and creative imagination. If I had been unable to get back to the reality of the lecture, and if my own private world had had an insistent urgency that took over direction of my behaviour, I could probably have been diagnosed as schizophrenic. So, although psychotic people are rejected because they do not make the usual relationship connections with other people, their experience may not be quite so alien as it seems.

Schizophrenic people have become lastingly disconnected from other people, as Nebuchadnezzar was. In this cut-off state, the social conscience disappears and is replaced by odd unintelligible behaviour that is either withdrawn or extravagant. There is disconnection both with one's fellow man and also with God, so that the person is trapped in a tormenting fate, and driven by distressing forces.[68] Normal social, cultural and spiritual relationships are no longer taken for granted but are called into question and reinterpreted. It is as though the person no longer belongs amongst us. But although the schizophrenic person has to "live with the animals among the plants of the earth", as it were, there is a remnant (described in Daniel 4:15 as a stump in the ground) of humanity in that person which remains alive with God's breath whilst there is life. The soul retains the potential to reconnect with other people. By God's grace and in

---

[68] The will loses its freedom due to oppressive spiritual forces that have managed to stultify it. These powers have therefore managed to control the person's accountability and level of responsibility. This has legal implications. No system of law can be sufficiently just to bring adequate peace unless it acknowledges that Almighty God is the eternal judge who has made it possible for people to be set free and unless individuals be held personally accountable.

due course, in a way that can once again make sufficient sense for there to be a return to sanity, that person can respond to the warmth of other human beings. If that person will call on God in the name of Jesus to change and to heal him, healing can become complete, for the Spirit of God bestows soundness of mind (2 Timothy 1:7 KJV).

Illustration

In order to illustrate how this disconnection may occur, I have created the following story which I hope will demonstrate the sort of events that might beguile human nature into a state of schizophrenia; and I have also tried to indicate how healing might be found.[69]

A young man of eighteen, from moderately prosperous family in a small rural village, decided to join the army. He had been to local schools but had not done very well and had few friends. Now he was restless and wanted to move away from home. His parents encouraged him to make an independent life for himself. He arrived at the barracks in a distant town with every intention to make a go of it.

But everything was very different here from the isolated community in which he had grown up. Within a few weeks he began to feel very unsure of himself. He started to worry about being unable to focus on what he was supposed to learn. His commitment to soldiering became ambivalent. He was expected to be self-reliant, but he was increasingly bewildered by army culture. He was expected to fight his corner and be clear about

---

[69]Although this is a composite description taken from many sources, it is inevitable that some people known to me may find resemblances to their own case. I apologise if anyone feels offended and I acknowledge my debt to all the people who have trusted me with intimate details of their lives. However, the details in this story are commonly found and it has not been my intention to refer to anyone in particular. There seems no better vehicle than a story to explain schizophrenia in ordinary terms so that people may discover greater faith for healing, and real hope.

what he thought and where he stood in many situations he had never faced before. There was not much room for doubt or confusion. Training was demanding.

Other people needed to rely on him, but he became increasingly reserved and unforthcoming. Taunts and curses from other young men frightened him. They seemed to have no understanding of his fear and indecision, and seemed to find his reactions strange. He hated himself for feeling so lonely. His attempts to speak with other recruits about his sensitive feelings and thoughts caused him to be mocked and ostracised; but when he did not speak about them at all, he became even more bewildered and frustrated. The young soldier's options seemed to be either to speak truthfully and be considered mad, or to remain silent and go mad. He was aware of being doomed either way.

His options became increasingly charged with desperation. It seemed he could lose his mind. He knew no one to rely on. He soon felt utterly stressed, exasperated, helpless, trapped, confused and overwhelmed by his circumstances. Unable to think clearly or make any decision, it began to seem that anything he attempted would fail. And within a few weeks he began to feel that his very life was hanging in the balance.[70]

Any true consideration of reality caused him unbearable panic and stress. Eventually his mind drifted much more into what might perhaps be the case rather than what actually was the case. It began to seem that some of his thoughts were being taken away by forces that were in control of his life, which then proceeded to

---

[70] The work on the "double bind" first done by Gregory Bateson and others in the middle of the twentieth century at the Veterans Administration Hospital, Palo Alto, California, remains significant. A person in a double bind will be rejected and invalidated either for speaking urgent truth or for denying it. If survival seems to depend on that truth, all seems lost. See Bateson, G., Jackson, D.D., Haley, J., Weakland, J., (1956) *Towards a Theory of Schizophrenia*, Behavioural Science, Vol.1, No.4. At this point normal communication with other people may be lost. But the one true God will provide a way out if you hear him through the Lord Jesus Christ (2 Kings 7:3-4, Psalm 142, 1 Corinthians 10:13).

comment upon his life and try to control him. A voice inside his head periodically commented that he was going to die. He was tormented by these voices and could not shake them off. He could not tell anyone about them without being ridiculed or condescended to. So he often did what they indicated, and mostly gave in to them. He ignored the fact that he found this oppressive.

Sometimes he was seen to be awake and wandering around at night when others were asleep. Other people began to be frightened of him. His language became vague and poetic, moving frequently from one set of facile imagery to another.

He often seemed to be in a sort of distressed, stultified trance. He felt intimidated, manipulated, dominated and controlled by personal and spiritual forces that for most other people seemed to be posing no threat at all. At the same time, in a desperate attempt to cling on to whatever personal autonomy he could muster, he tried to resist being totally overcome by forces that threatened to deprive him of any mind of his own by occasional outbursts of aggression.

The stresses of bewilderment caused him unwittingly to infer wrong meanings from other people's words and behaviour, and in secret panic his suppositions would sometimes be blown out of all proportion in wild flights of fantasy and imagination that were very real to him. So other people's reactions were sometimes seriously misunderstood. As his understanding became distorted a profound sense of dread threatened to force him to lose his mind and enter a sort of death.

He was suspicious and irritable, clinging on to life in a way that other people failed to understand. He became oversensitive and was offended by words that were not actually meant personally, and on occasion he became angry and defensive. It seemed very unsafe to let anyone close. He developed a few threatening mannerisms, and occasionally assumed odd postures. This behaviour seemed to have a private meaning.

His language became ever more cryptic and difficult to decipher. On a few occasions he had responded with a rage which terrified other people. He failed to bond with any others and naturally felt utterly lost.

Quite soon, he accepted that he could not cope, so he reported sick. He felt unable to make the doctors and nurses really understand. But he knew of no one else to turn to.

The young soldier was referred to a psychiatrist who diagnosed schizophrenia. Strong anti-psychotic sedative medication was prescribed – pills at first; injections after a few weeks. These drugs controlled his fear and other feelings, along with his thoughts and behaviour, but they made him feel rather rigid. Although he felt imprisoned in a chemical straitjacket he nevertheless took the pills and injections to save trouble. Within a few months he was discharged from the army on medical grounds.

He went home, and his parents were very worried about him. He was subdued. He could not find any paid work. He became apathetic. He said he had lost his feelings. His eyes revealed no hope. He accepted that he was ill, and so did they, with great sadness. But he made no attempt to discover any other sort of help. He was restless and uncomfortable at home. The distressed atmosphere was oppressive. So he moved out to a rented room in a boarding house in a town near the family home.

He regularly attended the psychiatric outpatient clinic at the local hospital. He passed the time of day with one or two other people he met at the clinic who seemed to have a similar condition, but they never tried to discover reasons for their predicament. The staff adjusted his medication and helped with some practical advice. He spent many empty hours watching television, smoking, wandering the streets, hanging about.

Understanding madness

It seems reasonable to postulate that he had been unable to discover sufficient sound sense[71] in order to find his way out of the muddle he found himself in after joining the army, because the circumstances of his life up until that time had not given him sufficient firm ground of security in his soul to meet his radically changed circumstances.[72]

His state after being diagnosed and medicated was so stultified that his autonomy was forfeited, and he was wide open to being controlled by whoever offered him cigarettes, food and shelter and by whatever happened next. He had lost courage and had lost all desire to overcome any of the forces of the world. Yet he did not have the insight to see how trapped he was, and how, frustrated, angry and hopeless.

People who become schizophrenic are desperately stressed in the very depths of their souls. They are pulled into hopelessness, even into fearing death, because there seems to be no way for their disorganised and fragmented responses to events to be made sense of with other people. The medication usually given controls extravagant behavioural effects of the stress. So the spirit becomes effectively crushed. There seems no way out. There seems to be no truth, and no way to get free, so no real life seems possible. A desperate sort of trance is induced in which they are internally torn between life and death, but compliant.

The angst of their internal arousal may make the messages of their demons so unusually vivid that they are heard as voices.

Unless the person accepts the redemption freely provided by Jesus Christ and seeks the kingdom of God, the heart will become darkened and the thinking increasingly futile. (Romans 1:21).

---

[71] *Sense* is from Latin *sentire* = to feel; *sentis* = a path (by which one feels one's way) (Partridge, E. (1966) *Origins*, London, Routledge & Kegan Paul).
[72] See my discussion of anxiety in Chapter 5 above. Ontological insecurity is usefully discussed by R D Laing (1960) in Chapter 3 of *The Divided Self*, London, Tavistock Publications (1959) Ltd.

Then the person will readily come to believe all sorts of deceptions and allow wickedness to take hold (2 Thessalonians 2:11, see also Psalm 95:10-11, Deuteronomy 28:20 and 28).

Sooner or later it is usually possible, for those with eyes to see, to discover that a person who becomes schizophrenic has had some hidden insecurity in the very foundations of the mind from an early age, usually from before the age of eight. Only rarely, however, is it possible to use this information for healing.

Sometimes the tendency to insecurity and confusion seems inherited. One way or another it will be possible to trace the insecurity to deception and denial of truth – even in past generations. The deception may have been unintentional but certainly it is not always so. It will commonly have resulted from events within the family that have been responded to with guilt, denials, lies, plausible excuses, threats, doubt, and confusion.

Matters that have not been brought into the light before God for his forgiveness and healing can cause all sorts of havoc. The wool will have been pulled over the child's eyes regarding the truth of particular significant events. The rest of the family may even refuse to acknowledge the fact. Thus beliefs, statements, attitudes and behaviours, inherited from family and built into the mind, may eventually fail to stand up to testing if circumstances radically change.

There may be a family history on the father's side, or on the mother's side, or both, that would explain why certain issues have been avoided and kept secret, perhaps something as shameful as incest, for example, or felony, or murder, or madness of unknown cause, or suicide, or shameful illness, or shameful death, or perhaps collusion in hidden activities, or membership of a powerful secret society, or the worship of a strange or forbidden deity. This will have resulted in the child from an early age taking as true faulty interpretations of relationships and events that in fact had different and perhaps more powerful significance than they have actually been believed to have had. In this sort of way the mind will have been built up on insecure foundations.

Accounting for the young man's state of mind

The fact is that this particular young soldier had been too much altogether for his family to cope with when he was born. His mother had struggled to cope with the pregnancy. Thereafter he was in effect rejected and neglected, despite their pretence to the contrary. Excess fuss and attention can sometimes hide guilt about lack of love. It seems reasonable to suppose that this could explain why he had always had a feeling that he was bad and would fail.

His father and mother had never told anyone that he had been conceived at a time when they were out of work and had no money and were struggling to nurse the mother's grandmother who was dying of tuberculosis. The family still harboured unspoken suspicions and resentments about this grandmother because she was secretly believed to have conceived the mother's mother through an incestuous relationship with her elder brother. Furthermore, that particular generation had been involved with spiritualism. They had persisted in trying to communicate with the dead. Demons had therefore controlled their lives. The man's mother had never really got free of this.

The shame of incest had tormented the soldier's mother's mother (the soldier's grandmother not his mother's) so much that she had spent many years in a psychiatric hospital and died there, before her time. Nursing the mother's grandmother, at the same time as coping with her pregnancy, had overburdened the family to such an extent that the young soldier's mother had felt unable to cope and had rejected him in her womb. A feeling that he was different from other people and did not really belong had persisted as he grew up.

His mother still felt unable to love him fully, although she had never been able to acknowledge this openly. She covered it up by trying to adopt a positive attitude. And although he always secretly felt that he was bad and wrong, he had never spoken of it, and had just tried to please everyone and keep the peace. The whole family had been nominally Christian and they had

177

resolved not to speak of negative or hurtful things. So these matters had never been put right with God. Instead the family had been determined to be respectable and successful and to put on a good face and be active in the church.

Because hidden matters had not been dealt with, their religion was rather legalistic and less vibrant and less real than it might have been. But this was hardly noticed in the church they attended because sin was no longer considered very seriously there, and it was not the fashion to ask the Holy Spirit to reveal personal matters that needed healing. They had a form of godliness but lacked the power (2 Timothy 3:5) and though they honoured God with their lips their hearts were often far from him (Isaiah 29:13).

The only way to be accepted within his family had been to obey the unspoken rules of respectability. He was the middle child of three, rather overshadowed by his two brothers, and had been expected to be successful at earning his living like everyone else. But very significant feelings had had to be denied, and he had never, in truth, been recognised for the unique individual he was. Nor had he ever been able to have much of a mind of his own. Although he did not really know why, he had always had a vague sense of being under some sort of duress. So he had wanted to get away, out of the rather deadening controls that had seemed to constrain him at home. Therefore he had decided to join the army. His true thoughts and feelings and abilities were hidden. They were a muddle in the dark. But until he joined the army he had managed to muddle through.

Healing

Three years after his discharge from the army, through family contacts, this young man started to attend a church where one of the elders eventually began to take a genuine interest in him. The young man found himself willing to trust him. He began to visit the elder's home for an hour once a week to work in the elder's vegetable garden and talk. The elder was able, by the grace of

God, to read between the lines of the cryptic shorthand of much of his facile, metaphorical language, so that he became aware of how worried, frightened, lost, angry and distressed the young man really was.

The elder quite enjoyed the sort of talk, common amongst schizophrenic people, in which the only way to address some apparently unapproachable subjects is by innuendo. This becomes a sort of poetry in which true meaning is only gleaned by those with ears to hear. "This vase is cracked; it will not hold water. The disdain of Satan constrains me," the young man had said one day, when looking at a flower pot. And the elder let him know that he believed he was indirectly indicating his apparent confusion, brokenness and powerlessness and sense of being controlled by the accusations of the devil. The young man found himself relieved to be heard. It made it possible to begin to feel real.

The older man was able to take the apparent muddle of what the young man said, consider it seriously and discover truth. But he did not go out of his way to be helpful. He gave the young man space to be responsible for himself. He just kept faith and was there when he said he would be there. He did not refuse to listen any more after the young man told him the birds in the field were watching him and mocking him by interfering with what he did. Nor did he flinch when the young man told him what his voices said.

When he acted strangely the older man just accepted it. Nor did he refuse to see him when the young man was unkempt and stinking. He took seriously Jesus' injunction not to condemn (Matthew 7:1). So the young man began to speak increasingly clearly about issues he had never previously realised were there to be opened up.[73] As matters came to light that had hitherto been hidden in the dark, so that he had not been conscious of them, he realised that when Jesus said he was the light of the world it was true. The Holy Spirit reveals truth about facts, and enables unspeakable matters to be spoken about. Because of the victory over Satan and sin and death that the Lord Jesus won on the cross, there is always hope for overcoming their suppression and for healing. Therefore it is safe with Jesus for such matters to come to light (Ephesians 5:6-14 and 1 John 1:7).

Being relieved to find someone genuine, he slowly began to make sense of his personal story. His hopelessness and confusion began to disappear. He found encouragement and began to make one or two friends. As truth dawned for the young man, and things began to make more sense, he recognised the living presence of God in the meetings he was having with the elder. He recognised that he could no longer go on in his own strength, and that there seemed no real guarantee of finding healing and sanity except through Jesus.

One day he got down on his knees in his room and turned to God and thanked him for Jesus. He confessed his sinfulness and that of his family and asked Jesus into his heart, and thanked him for becoming his personal saviour and lord.

Later he was baptised in water. Some time afterwards he found himself baptised in Holy Spirit - according to the promise in Matthew 3:11. And upon this rock he began to discover that his life could be well founded.

He knew God had forgiven him for his own sin, so he forgave the other people whom he now knew had sinned against him, and this gave him a real sense of new life. More of the truth about his ancestors came to light, and he forgave them. And he forgave his parents in detail, too. As time progressed, and as he changed,

---

[73] If a person is sure of being accepted, heard, safely loved, and not judged, he knows he can then stop hiding behind cryptic, bizarre and obfuscating language, even if he has been given a serious psychiatric diagnosis.

quite a few demons were expelled in the name of Jesus.[74] And he was delivered of the inherited influence of unclean spirits and cut free of ungodly controlling relationships with members of his family in the name of Jesus. Other relationships that had been wrong with God were put right, so he was no longer subject to intimidation, manipulation, domination or control by others.

His doctor eventually agreed gradually to reduce the medication, and after a year or two it was finally stopped. It has not been required again. As the truth of the past had dawned, he had made his peace with God about it and found healing.

He persevered to develop a sound mind of his own, and started reading Christian books. The elder carefully kept faith with him for several years, enjoying fellowship with him in a small group of Christians who met weekly in a house group, and also meeting with him privately.

Occasionally it became possible to unravel profound personal issues. Often they prayed together. Occasionally demons were expelled. It was not always easy. At first the elder had often felt buffeted and deeply troubled within his own soul by the young man's inarticulate emotion and pain and demons, until one day the young man had come to realise that the painful fear that something terrible would happen, and that he would lose control of his mind and die, was no longer there. Only after that did he become calmer. Only after that did others stop feeling their empathetic hearts being bashed about in his presence.

He found work after a couple of years. Later he discovered great compassion in his heart for other people who were suffering as he had, and God gave him opportunities to help them find release.

---

[74] *Pigs in the Parlour* by Frank & Ida Mae Hammond (1973, Kirkwood, Mo., Impact Books) is helpful, including the chapter on Schizophrenia. As they describe, demonic forces may effectively spin the lost person in a vortex. Other books on deliverance are listed in the Bibliography. In addition to deliverance the mind needs to be renewed through validating the truth of experience (John 13:14).

Reflections

Being psychotic is the loneliest place on earth and it can be hard work to get free. The condition is precipitated by being caught in all sorts of weird hidden deceptions, being faced with accusation, curses and rejection, and remaining hopeless. Through no fault of your own you have become stultified.

The way out to abundant, meaningful life is to allow the living God to reveal his truth and show you the way. This means asking the Lord Jesus Christ, to save you. If you will accept that Jesus paid the price for your sin when he died on the cross, and that he rose from the dead the third day, and if you will ask God to send the Holy Spirit to guide you, he certainly will. Something new will begin, and your life will never be the same again (2 Corinthians 5:17). It will be best to have some human being to rely on (Romans 10:14). Then you can begin to find your way in this world to being free to understand and be understood, and to love and be loved sincerely and truthfully.

The "old self", your unregenerate personality, must receive and digest the words of the Holy Spirit before the "new self" can be reborn in Jesus (as in Colossians 3:9-10). This is a process in which we need other people in order to progress and mature. The people who help you do not have to be perfect and understand everything. The important thing is for the afflicted person to be able to be held in genuine, sincere relationship with at least one other person, and in the love and truth of God, so that enough hope and faith may be found for the reality of God's kingdom to be discovered in this world in which we have to live.

Such good-enough relationship only really comes from one source, who is the one true God of Abraham, Isaac and Jacob, whom Jesus knew as his Father, and who works through his people. Being held in godly love and sincerity amongst people who are not blood family, whilst you open up your madness into Jesus' light can succeed in bringing you back to life in this world, and in giving you enough sense to find your way again. But the only person you can absolutely rely on for your healing is the

Lord Jesus Christ of Nazareth. He is the way to the God who heals. And every one of us needs to be constantly purified by the application of his redeeming blood (1 John 1:7).

Beware
There are some Christians who will believe it is only God who can save a person and that faithful fellowship with other people, as they work free of sensitive issues of their personal lives, is unnecessary. They believe there is nothing much other people can actually do, and that helping others like this can cause trouble for Christians and lead them into sin. They believe, therefore, that it is best not to become too involved with other people who are in a mess. They adhere to the belief that is right only to preach the Gospel and teach God's word, and then leave it all to God.

Indeed, the lot of many people does often seem very hopeless. Other people can be very disturbing. Redemption and salvation are quite obviously supernatural works of the living God. And you can lead a horse to water but you cannot make him drink, as they say.

The presence of the living God in his people heals
But people with the Holy Spirit living in them have warm hearts that care, with godly wisdom. They become concerned about their neighbours through the love of God. And they introduce the Spirit of truth as they speak about what is going on using words full of the grace of God, seasoned with salt (Colossians 4:6). So through their actions and relationships the light of God comes into the world, and the person of Jesus is revealed. Holy Spirit living in a person can be infectious.

People can catch Holy Spirit as folk rub shoulders with one another in the nitty-gritty of real everyday concerns. But he is less likely to be known, because he will seem less relevant, if significant issues are being covered up.

Another human being can often hold a person through keeping good faith whist they are vulnerable, too, much as a parent holds a child. Provided there is no deception (Matthew 23:8-11), and provided it is realised that there is work to be done to get free through the relationship, this sort of discipleship, one person present for another, seems to me to be very necessary. An added bonus for people who help others like this is that finding healing for the distress other people cause you can, through God's grace, draw you closer to the Lord.[75]

Freak-out

It is worth mentioning that although this sort of healing process is most commonly gradual, there are occasions when much of the work may be done in a very short time in a crisis, or freak-out, in which a person has many vivid experiences and understands new meanings with startling rapidity – rather like Paul's experiences recorded in Acts 9.

For a crisis to be truly healing, as it was for Paul, it is necessary for the afflicted person to know the Lord God of Israel and to have a living relationship with him and to be appealing to him for healing. It is also necessary to have a safe house, such as the house of Judas on Straight Street in Damascus turned out to be for Paul, preferably with plenty of constant discerning people around to surround it with as much prayer and practical support as possible.

In the days before anti-psychotic drugs were invented this sort of thing was a more frequent occurrence, but it can still happen today and may occasionally provide quick resolution of torment when a person is utterly in bits. [76] There may be a vast reformation of the mind as the higher authority of God is

---

[75] I have personally laboured amongst the hardest cases and certainly have never come to believe anyone to be beyond redemption. My persuasion is Arminian rather than Reformed or Calvinist.

[76] Anton Boisen was able to use psychiatric hospitals for several such crises in the days before the drug chlorpromazine was invented. He was a Christian and one of his books, *The Exploration of the Inner World,* describes this, and is listed in the Bibliography. Other examples mostly go unrecorded.

accepted into areas that have hitherto been confused or in the dark.

Spiritual crises like these do not usually last more than about two weeks, sometimes much less, provided they are not interfered with, and provided drugs do not become necessary because of serious and obvious danger. Unless there is a real personal relationship with the one true God of Christians, who is the God of Israel, permanent relief from torment may not come, however, although there will be some healing if truth and love and authentic empathy get through to the afflicted person.

Family secrets

As truth dawns, uncomfortable facts may emerge into the light and sometimes families may do all they can to make sure that these facts should not become known. Such family secrets can sometimes keep people trapped in a schizophrenic existence, and this sort of thing is one of the main obstacles to the healing of mental illness.

Families may contradict or deny the truth, or use more complicated deceptions to prevent the truth from emerging, and so maintain the cover-up in the guise of respectability, as though any other course could drive them all mad. Shame about having someone mentally ill in the family may be found to obscure a lack of willingness or an inability to discover truth about family myths, so that the mentally ill person effectively becomes the family scapegoat.

The schizophrenic person may sometimes have been so frightened, hopeless, indoctrinated with deception, and lacking in faith, as to prefer to believe the family version of events and remain under the domination of the old family controls, and may therefore remain confused and trapped by double meanings, innuendo and apparent threats which hide truth that no one will speak about or recognise. Freedom may then actually seem too terrifying a prospect. Even Christian families will behave like this.

Family deceptions and secrets only become apparent when they come into the light. Jesus is the true light. What is hidden may remain in the dark until Jesus comes. People who want to keep things in the dark may actually be found secretly to hate Jesus (John 1:5). Furthermore, schizophrenia, or other tormenting resistance to truth, may get worse as the light threatens to penetrate hidden secrets, until peace is made with the living God through Jesus. The old English proverb which says, "It is always darkest just before the dawn," may seem very relevant.

For the person receiving God's healing it will most probably, therefore, be necessary for some person who is independent of the family to be available, with whom to keep faith for a good long time. Although it may well be that the whole family seems to need healing, an individual may have to leave the family in order to work free (Mark 3:21 and 31-35). It will prove to be necessary for most schizophrenic people who seek healing to find hospitality somewhere away from home.

Nevertheless, if a miracle should occur so that the whole family actually seeks healing because one of its members seems schizophrenic, all those family members should be willing to hear unpalatable words in the presence and the love of God. And they will need to be willing generously to accept that meanings may sometimes be distorted by pent-up emotion which needs to be brought before God's throne and taken to the cross.

The suffering of one family member is bound to affect the others deeply (1 Corinthians 12:26); and so also may the healing. This can be a very painful process, and if the senior male in the family cannot, for whatever reason, be granted a place of godly authority by the schizophrenic person (1 Corinthians 11:3), that afflicted person will need individual help from outside the family.

So the whole family will need the self-discipline to wait on God, to face the truth, to forgive and be forgiven, and to persevere to find his peace. What has been going on within the family will be part of what has produced the sickness of the one person. Past family history, including the skeletons in the cupboard and everything that has been swept under the carpet for generations, and wrong worship, and other wrong relationships, should all be brought truthfully before God for his healing. Wrongful deceptions and accusations, often repeated through innuendo and miscommunication, will come to light through the activity of the Holy Spirit, and be clarified and healed.

It is an irrelevance to cast blame upon families, however, because the interpersonal bonds within families, particularly the blood bond that began in the womb of the mother, are foundational. Family is God's provision for rearing the young; and removing a child from a family inevitably creates deep wounds of rejection, no matter how bad the family may seem.

Around the time of adolescence is about the earliest a young person is really capable of becoming aware that there could perhaps be another, better family, namely the family of God. And even then, those who reckon themselves part of the family of God are usually less than perfect. But we should take note that the Lord Jesus found it necessary to leave his family (Mark 3:21 and 31-35), and he taught that the kingdom family of God his Father must come first (Luke 14:26). Christians are encouraged in Scripture to be hospitable (Romans 12:13) and God promises to set the lonely in families (Psalm 68:6). Furthermore, Jesus did not come to condemn us but to save us (John 3:17) and God requires repentance in the light of his truth (John 8:31-32) and he offers healing.

No obvious family dynamics

Finally, in those few instances in which family issues do not seem to have predominated, it will be necessary to deal with the roots of fear and fantasy, and of bitterness and rejection. Ambivalence and pagan spirituality may also be an issue. And it will be necessary to work out how such influences came to play such a powerful role. Particularly confusing and overwhelming circumstances will need to be brought before the Lord. Then there can be forgiveness, change and healing.

Chronic schizophrenia

The young man whose story was related above providentially met someone through whom to find healing fairly early in the course of his affliction. However, there are many people who never realise that true healing can come through the Lord Jesus Christ. Consequently they allow themselves to be treated according to their symptoms, that is, according to the classifiable abnormalities objectively observed by scientific professionals whose job is to manage the condition rather than speculate about healing.

So they may never find anyone with whom to begin to speak openly without feeling a need to be excessively defensive and obscure. They remain chronically wounded and demonized, and seem incapable of real meeting.

The chronic course of schizophrenia is thus complicated by disguised despondency, in which the schizophrenic person effectively accepts the curse of madness (Deuteronomy 28:28) and exists cocooned within the sorcery of prescribed medication, which stops the feelings and hinders true accountability. Having accepted the diagnosis they are resigned to avoiding responsibility for themselves and living on hand-outs. Periodically the original stress, confusion and madness will inevitably be triggered by external circumstances, so the person is trapped in medication and hospitalization. Truth is hidden. The will becomes weak and the spirit is effectively crushed.

This is by no means always the fault of the psychiatrists and psychologists and nurses and social workers who have been called upon for help, for the only help that will be effective is what the schizophrenic person can be persuaded to put up with. Living faith is usually lost and most people put their confidence in scientific medicine and psychology.[77] Only very few will retain any faith in a person, or in the person of God. Furthermore, it can be painful to open up wounded parts of the soul that have been dormant for years. And some people seem to have no concept of truth at all, and many are put off accepting faithful, disinterested godly truth and love because of personal prejudices about the people who offer it. So after many hopeless years, chronically schizophrenic people will mostly have abandoned their lives to the desolation of opportunistic meaninglessness with medication.[78]

Just a few may want something to be done to heal their wretchedness. They may not realise, however, that it is possible for them to have faith in the God of Israel and engage in a healing process with people who know him, people who are different from the people to whom they have cynically become accustomed. Those schizophrenic people whom God is touching will be missed unless Christians understand how God may use new human relationships to heal them.

Medication

Drugs are usually necessary to hold the person safe if it is likely that harm would result from loss of self-control. They may be useful for holding a person chemically until sufficient self-control returns. People use drugs to hold themselves together when they cannot articulate what is in the dark to bring it into the light. And most drugs used for schizophrenia seem to control the emotions of insecurity and fear.

Drugs, however, do not do the healing, although they may be said to offer a cure.

---

77 When you are living in absolute hell you would take anything you can to stop it, so drugs are very seductive and it can be hard to have faith in anything else. After all, whom can you trust?

78 Goffman, E. (1961) *Asylums*. New York, Anchor Books.

Healing begins through relationships that shed light on hidden issues. Much healing can often be accomplished, however, whilst the person continues to take regular medication.

Scientific psychiatry

The fashionable way to avoid painful family soul-searching is to insist that schizophrenia is a physical illness. Those who prefer to remain within the confines of physical science and who describe schizophrenia as a neuro-developmental disorder, and who quote neuroimaging studies and neurophysiological studies and the results of psychometric tests and genetic studies, are not wrong. However, the results of neuroimaging and neurophysiological studies, and psychometrics, and all the other scientific investigations, are probably most truthfully interpreted as the consequences of the condition rather than the cause.

The most notable studies of genetic inheritance quoted in standard medical textbooks show that children of schizophrenic parents may possibly develop schizophrenia even if removed from their parents at birth. However, such studies should probably be viewed in the light of the probability that what we do affects our genes just as much as our genes affect what we do.[79] Templates for patterns of behaviour are actively laid down in the living body (probably in ribonucleic acid formations) when experience counts, and behaviour patterns may thus be inherited and remembered through genes. Genes are part of the living body, part of the soul, not just inert unchangeable structures in a mechanical body.[80] Genetic material is being laid down all the time, and is inherited. Therefore genetic inheritance is susceptible to healing change, by the grace of God, if people will accept total responsibility for themselves, including all they have inherited

---

[79] Chief Rabbi Sir Jonathan Sacks said this on BBC radio in 2007, and my own experience leads me to agree.
[80] See the diagram of *Soul* at the end of Chapter 2 of my book *Healing for the Wounded Life*.

genetically, and make themselves accountable to God, and be reconciled to him. Schizophrenic tendencies, and tendencies to other sicknesses such as coronary artery disease and diabetes, are similarly inherited; but it is significant that no single gene has been found responsible for this sort of inheritance.

In the medical textbooks schizophrenia is defined as a disorder characterised by distortions of thinking, feeling and perception, whilst clear consciousness and intellectual capacity are maintained. Hallucinations and delusions are common, and behaviour may be erratic or even dangerous. The course of the sickness may be episodic or continuous. The diagnosis is imprecise and describes a generalised picture, and each individual case is different.

For administrative purposes, and in view of the fact that the incidence is about four per thousand, necessitating the provision of an enormous number of hospital beds, etc.,[81] it is expedient to classify the various manifestations of schizophrenia into paranoid, hebephrenic, catatonic, etc., and to describe the chronic course of the unhealed affliction in detail.

According to this classification, <u>paranoia</u> describes delusions of persecution. Those who have eyes to see may discern that love will have been rejected with implicit accusations, causing deep wounds in the soul, with denied guilt, and with aggression. Therefore significant love impulses will be fought off. There will be over-sensitivity and suspicion with extravagant retaliation and probably some crazy delusions and hallucinations.

<u>Hebephrenia</u> describes the erratic, emotional, irresponsible, sometimes grossly extravagant and confused behaviour of a schizophrenic person refusing to be subdued into hopelessness.

<u>Catatonia</u> describes constrained attitudes with excitement or stupor, mannerisms and posturing, including remaining in one position for a long time. To the discerning, the soul may be seen

---

[81] Psychiatry takes about 12% of the National Health budget in the UK, more than any other speciality.

to be in absolute anguish, so that any physical movement could compromise the person. Yet occasionally a catatonic person can be released through warm authentic responses from the presence another individual.

Humanistic, scientific ways of trying to classify, describe and understand schizophrenia do not, however, reveal the full spiritual dimension from the Christian point of view. Therefore they are unable to show the way to true healing.

Although the world says schizophrenia needs heavy drug treatment, my experience is that the first priority is some mutual recognition and understanding with another member of the human race who is willing, preferably through the power of the Holy Spirit, to love his neighbour as himself, because this begins to remove the pain for which the drugs are given. In other words, the first priority is reconnection with the human race through the love and the truth of God.

9

ORGANIC PSYCHIATRIC CONDITIONS

It is prudent to be alert to the possibility that distressing states of mind, or strangely incongruent behaviour, may have a physical cause that should receive specialist medical intervention. For example, altered states of consciousness, disorders of thinking, loss of emotional control, memory defects and personality change can all be produced by injuries to the head. They can also be caused by degenerative disease, by infections, by physiological deficiencies, by tumours, or by intoxication. In all these sorts of conditions there is physiological or structural damage to the brain that could perhaps be made less harmful by being treated with medical technology.

This is not a scientific textbook and this chapter is only a summary, included for the sake of proper perspective, emphasising salient and cautionary points for those who are involved, one way or another, in Christian ministry.

Most of what is generally referred to as mental illness involves the soul much more than the body. And although sicknesses of mind and soul always produce concurrent physiological changes in the living body, they do not produce gross physical pathology, and they are therefore not described as "organic." However, there are a multitude of organic conditions that may mimic mental illnesses of the soul. So it is necessary to be discerning, although it is rare for organic conditions not to be obvious.

Certainly if, after getting to know the person well with the Lord and searching for all possible roots of the trouble, there should be any sense that there seems to be no logical explanation for a condition, medical opinion should be sought. But although technological medical intervention is appropriate in some mental illness, by no means is it necessary in all. Sickness of the soul that is not organic may more logically be considered to be the business of spiritual authorities.

We shall begin this summary of organic mental illness with childhood and we shall progress to old age. It will not be totally inclusive.

Congenital factors

The brain of a baby may be damaged by congenital factors of several sorts. A condition may cause early death, or may persist to hinder normal development. It may be genetic, although there may or may not be firm evidence that it has been inherited. Genes occasionally mutate, and environmental factors affecting the mother, such as infection, drugs, trauma, malnutrition, irradiation, and (if we have the eyes to see this) spiritual influences as well, may interfere with the natural development of the child in the womb. Sometimes the reasons why development does not seem to have proceeded ideally will remain unknown.

Congenital problems – not only involving the brain but also including every sort of abnormality - occur in about one in fifty births, and they account for at least one in ten infant deaths. Some of these conditions continue to retard the normal processes of development as the child grows up, and they may cause learning difficulties. Parents may slowly realise that the child is relatively unresponsive, or slow. There may be unusual delay in reaching normal milestones of development. In some conditions the child may be irritable or have epileptic fits – and the congenital condition may or may not be the cause of the epilepsy. The practical difficulties of coping with the extra attention the child needs may cause distress. Furthermore, the parents may feel ashamed or even guilty for having had an unusual child and so they may reject the child. Although they may often try to hide such feelings, the child will nevertheless naturally pick them up. Consequent feelings of rejection in the child can generate other emotional difficulties such as anger and frustration and antisocial behaviour. Eventually the child may be sent to live in some sort of institutional setting. But it does not always have to be like this, and God will provide a way for people to live with difficult and unusual situations if he is asked to do so in the name of Jesus. Furthermore, he will show people how to die peacefully when the time comes, even if death seems premature (Psalm 68:6).

Many of people with congenital problems learn to adapt well to their disabilities, however, and many lead fruitful lives that are a blessing to others.

Congenital conditions with a genetic basis that may cause some degree of mental deficiency are: Down's syndrome, hydrocephaly, tuberous sclerosis, hypertelorism, microcephaly, craniostenosis. There are other congenital anomalies of the brain, too, notably those due to brain injury at birth. If oxygenated blood does not get to the brain or to parts of the brain in sufficient time, anoxia may kill off sensitive brain tissue. Medical intervention is usually not very effective for any of these conditions.

There are also many genetic metabolic disorders that a child may be born with that can cause an abnormal accumulation of substances in the tissues of the brain and other organs, thus interfering with normal functioning, such as galactosaemia (an example of a disorder of carbohydrate metabolism), phenylketonuria (an example of a disorder of amino-acid metabolism), Gaucher's disease (an example of a disorder of lipid metabolism), Wilson's disease (an example of a disorder of mineral metabolism), and so on. These disorders usually affect the physical appearance to some extent. Although many of these children die young, there is some effective medical treatment for some of these conditions, particularly if they can be diagnosed early.

Kernicterus, due to the poisonous effect of unconjugated bilirubin in the basal ganglia of the brain, which may be due to rhesus incompatibility although there are other causes, will also impair intelligence; but strenuous efforts are made in midwifery to reduce the incidence of this condition.

There are several different sorts of <u>porphyria</u> that are inherited and that may manifest in adult life with acute pains, emotional disturbance, confusion, hallucinations. Porphyria is due to an inherited defect in the pigment haem. King George III has been thought to have had porphyria.

<u>Huntington's disease</u> is also a congenital condition. But it only manifests in adult life. It is described below, under 'dementia'.

<u>Infections in the womb</u>, such as <u>rubella</u>, <u>syphilis</u>, <u>tuberculosis</u>, <u>toxoplasmosis</u>, and <u>cytomegalovirus</u> <u>infection</u>, may also produce mental retardation. Furthermore, <u>malnutrition</u> (perhaps due to <u>toxaemia</u> <u>of pregnancy</u>) or a mother's <u>drug taking</u> (including tobacco smoking) or <u>irradiation</u> may cause her baby not to grow as well as it should in the womb and this may cause some degree of impairment of intelligence in the child.

There are also disorders of hormone function that will be manifest shortly after birth, such as <u>thyroid deficiency</u>, and also <u>diabetes insipidus</u>. Unless these are quickly treated, they too can produce brain damage that retards development.

In addition, there are two conditions that may mimic a more severe condition by causing a child to be unable to learn to speak. The baby just may be suffering from <u>congenital deafness</u>, which may prevent the development of speech unless it is picked up in time; or <u>cerebral palsy</u>[82] (due to trauma, infection, kernicterus, hypoglycaemia, etc.) which may only be affecting speech and be giving a false impression that there are other deficiencies. Therefore it is necessary for a child who is not beginning to repeat the odd word at about twelve months of age to be examined by a doctor and recommended for remedial therapy if appropriate.

---

[82] Cerebral palsy is involuntary loss of muscle control as a result of damage to the brain. There may also be increase or decrease of muscle tone, involuntary movements, or epilepsy. It may be improved with physiotherapy.

Later factors

As a child grows up, and also in adulthood, <u>brain tissue may be damaged</u> by <u>physical injuries</u>, <u>tumours</u>, <u>infections</u>, and <u>degenerative diseases</u>, and by various <u>deficiencies</u>, <u>poisonings</u> and <u>intoxications</u>. These may give rise to disturbances of perception, thought, mood or behaviour, or to delirium, epilepsy, amnesia or dementia.

Intoxicants

Personal biochemistry may particularly be changed by ingested <u>drugs and intoxicants</u>, whether they are legally prescribed or illegal. Depending on the effects these substances have in the brain, they may distort the interpretation of events past and present. Thus they will distort the sense and meaning given to events, the responses to events, and the imagination. If used habitually for a long time they may distort the whole expression of personality. Furthermore, drugs and intoxicants affecting the brain may distort the censor. The censor focuses the attention on personal matter in hand, and cuts out extraneous factors from consideration. It was argued in Chapter 2 that censorship of what we perceive and do is a spiritually directed process involving the soul and the living physiology of the body; so when drugs change the physiology, the way the censorship works may be changed.

Thus hallucinogenic drugs like <u>LSD</u>[83] and <u>cannabis</u> can be seen to remove some restraint on the selection of sensory information, allowing the censor to be overwhelmed so that a flood of sensation comes into awareness. Thus the drug makes the person

---

[83] Lysergic acid diethylamide.

perceive more than may be adequately coped with.[84] And so an individual can become entranced more easily through the effects of these drugs. Natural attempts to make sense of all the information, and to give meaning to it all, and remember it, will depend on individual maturity.[85] The drugs impair judgement and excite capricious flights of fancy, and immature people can become uneasy, confused and frightened. Most people do not have the sophistication to cope adequately with the mind-blowing effects of these drugs.

Stimulants like <u>amphetamines</u> and <u>cocaine</u> increase excitement and increase the intensity of concentration. If too much is taken, they cause hyperactivity and restlessness. Habitual use helps to make a person insensitive, hard-hearted and inclined to be violent. Furthermore, illegal drug use distorts the conscience. Adrenalin addicts are full of pride and enjoy the excitement of rebellion.

<u>Alcohol</u> relaxes and disinhibits, and is both sedative and stimulant. In reasonable moderation it has always been enjoyed; but in excess it can depress physiological function, and in gross excess it depresses bodily function to such an extent that a bottle of spirits swallowed in one fell swoop can kill.

Sedatives like <u>diazepam</u> induce general relaxation and reduce anxiety and attentiveness, and they tend eventually to make people rather apathetic. Such drugs bring peace only as the world gives, not as God gives (John 14:27). <u>Morphine</u> and its derivatives, such as <u>heroin,</u> <u>pethidine,</u> <u>codeine</u> and <u>Methadone,</u> induce detachment, analgesia and euphoria, as well as making the person constipated. People very easily become addicted to

---

[84] Although many people believe the most significant consideration is the chemistry, the fundamental existential factor is what these drugs do to personal experience and relationships. So I am not going to attempt to describe drug chemistry. If you research it, you may discover the chemical concomitants of the experience. But that is not relevant to our discussion.

[85] The best estimate of maturity is how much godly wisdom the person has been able to embody as a result of experience, and from the riches of God's grace.

anaesthetic drugs like these in order to reduce the pain of contact with this world and substitute pleasant dreams.

You can become addicted to just about anything but these drugs, which take away the pain of physical and mental suffering, can be excessively attractive to people who cannot stand it any longer. It can soon seem impossible to stop taking the drug. Then ruthless priority in life is given to obtaining the next supply. Interest is lost in work, in health, in family and friends, and total focus fixes on the next fix.

Withdrawal from a drug habit can be extremely stressful. Not only does the body suddenly have to readjust to pain, but strongly ingrained patterns of thinking and behaviour have to change. There may be trembling, gut and bowel problems, memory problems, extravagant emotionalism, delirium, delusions, hallucinations, and secretive and disruptive antisocial behaviour..

Antidepressants make people feel less sad and anxious by enhancing the feeling of well-being. Antipsychotic drugs reduce the stress of extremes of angst, fear, rage, and so they artificially increase the level of censorship, cutting out stress-producing connections within the brain and thus controlling hallucinations, delusions and behaviour. Both these groups of drugs alter the biochemistry at the connecting points of nerves in the brain, and in this way artificially control the reactions and responses of the person, and hide the vulnerability. This may sometimes prevent relevant issues from being brought into the Lord's light for his healing. And chronic usage of these drugs always eventually changes the personality. If there is to be healing, it will be necessary to reduce the dose and eventually stop the drug altogether, provided it is safe to do so.

There are other drugs, too, for example grossly excessive doses of steroids, that may occasionally actually precipitate mental illness which can sometimes persist to become chronic. It is always worth checking whether or not drugs being taken may be the cause of any condition.

It is not uncommon for apathetic, distressed and rebellious people indiscriminately to mix drugs and take drug cocktails that cause them to behave in ways that alarm other people, so as to have exciting new experiences. When they are badly intoxicated such people will be living in a rather inaccessible world of their own and need protecting and watching to make sure they continue to breathe. They need access to water and toilet, and a modicum of human contact to put them in touch with reality, until they become sober.

Delirium

Delirium is clouding of consciousness, loss of vigilance, of attentiveness, and of awareness, with confusion and frequent restlessness, and loss of accustomed cognitive connections between memory, perception, judgement, comprehension, creative thinking, learning ability, and language. Emotional responses may be disinhibited and sometimes behaviour may very easily become extravagant, even violent, due to confusion, fear and frustration. Quiet familiar surroundings, genuine kindness and gentleness, and careful attention to nutrition and to excretory needs, will tend to reduce the stress and therefore calm the person.

Delirium is most commonly due either to poisoning, disease or head injury. A poisonous level of intoxication with alcohol is the most frequent cause. Withdrawal from other substances, notably opiates, hypnotics, and inhaled volatile solvents, may cause a fairly similar picture.

Withdrawal from heavy alcohol intoxication is called <u>delirium tremens</u>. Confusion and agitation are accompanied by shakiness, and sometimes by frightening hallucinations or epileptic fits, so it may be necessary for special sedation to be prescribed by a doctor.

Degenerative diseases of the brain which also cause dementia may occasionally give rise to delirium too – diseases such as <u>Alzheimers</u> disease, <u>Creutzfeld-Jacob</u> disease, etc. Delirium may also be caused by a disease process involving the whole person, such as a serious infection with high fever (e.g. typhoid, or septicaemia). It may also be caused by lack of oxygen in the blood (e.g. in chronic lung disease), or to liver failure, or to porphyria, or to failure of the adrenal, thyroid, pituitary or pancreatic endocrine glands (hypothyroidism, diabetes, etc.), or severe deficiency of B vitamins (pernicious anaemia, Korsakoff's syndrome, pellagra), or even lead poisoning.

Head injury
After a head injury with concussion there may be a period of unconsciousness which may only be transitory, or which may be much more prolonged. Depending on the severity of the trauma, there may or may not be damage to nerve cells that affect cognitive processes and behaviour. The severity of the concussion may be estimated by the extent of memory loss: in slight concussion memory loss lasts less than one hour but in very severe concussion there will be loss of memory (for events both before and after the injury) lasting more than seven days after the injury.

Before clear consciousness and memory recover, there may be a period of delirium, during which careful, peaceful nursing will greatly assist healing. As time goes on, after return to normal, there may eventually be much more recovery of memory for events before the injury than for events between the injury and "coming to".

Boxers, who may have been concussed with unusual frequency, sometimes become punch drunk, becoming rather slower mentally than they used to be, and a little ataxic with rather slurred speech.

The physical shock of concussion may leave a person for a very long time with headaches, giddiness, poor concentration, tiredness, irritability, forgetfulness, and apprehension, without any obvious physical pathology. These symptoms are signs of chronic stress from the shock, and they are sometimes somewhat relieved if financial compensation is received for the injuries. They may also respond to prayer for healing in the name of Jesus.

Physical injury to the head may cause damage to the tissues of the brain that proves to be permanently disabling. Occasionally severe head injury occurs during birth and can be the cause of cerebral palsy, mentioned above. But such injuries may occur at any age. Slow bleeding from a ruptured blood vessel may lead to a haematoma inside the skull, which may prolong the period of unconsciousness or prevent complete recovery from delirium. There may be a state of fluctuating degrees of confusion and slow deterioration of cognitive abilities. The diagnosis can easily be missed and the condition mistaken for depression or dementia. Surgery can sometimes save the person's life.

Head injuries that damage particular parts of the brain, often involving fractures of the skull from bullets or shrapnel, can cause changes to the personality that relate to the specific function of the damaged nervous tissue, in addition to the post-traumatic stress disorder, mentioned below. So injuries to the frontal lobes may make a person less sensitive, less creative, less curious, and more apathetic and euphoric. Injuries to the parietal lobes may cause neglect of parts of the body, difficulty recognising things, or inability to do certain things. Injuries to the temporal lobes may affect memory or the ability to recognise and find the right words.

Brain tumour

The effect of a tumour inside the skull is often not unlike that of a haematoma or brain injury. Parts of the brain are prevented from working properly as the tumour grows and, in consequence, there are often clinical signs, such as sensory or motor malfunction, incorrigible worry, or change of personality. The nature of the malfunction may help to determine the site of the tumour. However, some parts of the brain do not produce obvious signs when they are damaged; and so if no logical cause can be found for a person's distress, careful medical investigations should be undertaken. I well remember an intelligent woman who suffered inexplicable anxiety inside whose head we eventually discovered a cancer. There had been no other symptom. And I remember a man who had lived for a long time in a chronic ward of a psychiatric hospital, with a mistaken diagnosis of schizophrenia, who complained of gremlins in his head and whose behaviour was irritable, frustrated and difficult, who turned out eventually to have a large meningioma. Although tumours are relatively rare, they are a trap for the unwary. Attendants need to be vigilant and, if in doubt, they should seek specialist neurological, psychiatric and psychological opinions. Even then, sadly, mistakes will occasionally be made.

Epilepsy

Temporal lobe lesions may cause <u>temporal lobe epilepsy</u> (which is often due to birth trauma) in which normal activity suddenly stops and a state of fugue begins, with an aura of anxiety or a strange sensation in the stomach, throat or nose, or odd twisting movements of the mouth or limbs, followed by complex feeling and thinking states, sometimes with a sense of déjà vu, or with hallucinations, and automatic behaviour which may be emotionally charged. There is usually no memory of what happens during the fit.

Classically, <u>grand mal epileptic fits</u> follow a pattern of a warning aura, then a grunt or cry as the person falls, then the muscles of the whole body go into spasm. This lasts about half a minute and then the limbs are rapidly flexed and extended forcefully, and may be injured, and urine, and sometimes faeces, are passed involuntarily. These convulsions last about three minutes, decreasing in intensity and frequency. Then there is a short period of unresponsive coma, followed by sleep which may last several hours. Rarely the person may do things automatically (e.g. walking or undressing) for which there is afterwards no recollection.

When fits are frequent and not well controlled by drugs, or when people with severe brain injuries need extensive time and energy to be given by others to their special care, the social restrictions may cause hidden resentment and misery, and result in family disruption. In consequence, the afflicted person may suffer personality changes and become hopeless, or even obsessional, with stressed and disordered thinking. Prolonged sensitive, patient and practical help is required from many people with different skills. Carers will need prayerful support.

If the epilepsy was caused by injury, healing for the wounds in the name of the Lord Jesus may prove possible. In some instances deliverance from a spirit of epilepsy has been effective.

Shock

A shocking event may or may not be accompanied by physical trauma. Physical wounds will not only stress the body but will also shock the soul to a greater or lesser extent.

Severe physical wounds accompanied by severe shock may lead to eventual death. Such people need as much help as practical to die in peace. In war, or during a catastrophe, a careful degree of ruthlessness may be necessary in order to avoid wasting valuable time treating people who are likely to die. This is triage. Time and energy will be best used helping those in a more hopeful condition.

When the soul (which is the living principle within the body) is shocked, whether by physical trauma, or by other overwhelming events which shock the mind, the trauma is nevertheless mediated physiologically and biochemically. Stress hormones are released. It has been assumed that there must also be minute disruption of nerve connections. Vital energy becomes depleted.

Whilst attention is given to physical injury, it is necessary to be aware of how vulnerable the mind and soul of the shocked person will have become. The mind will be open to all sorts of impressions. Usual censorship defences will be overwhelmed and out of action. Therefore the healing environment should never be challenging. Quietness and attentive kindness assist healing (Luke 10:25-37).

Terrible events that overawe and overwhelm perception can inhibit the central nervous system, as described in Chapters 2 and 7. The person may be relatively unresponsive. They may also be excessively responsive to minor irritations. They may even go berserk. Restraint, if necessary, should be applied firmly, but as gently as possible.

The effects of unhealed shock can be persistent, as seen in <u>post-traumatic stress disorder</u>. A person may be left to cope not only with physical injury but also with flashback memories and sudden emotional reactions triggered by odd events. Because of the chronic stress of trying to hold the self together, resilience gives way to exhaustion. Forgetfulness, and splitting up of aspects of the personality, make coping with any change excessively stressful.

Healing of the shock in the name of Jesus may take time and involve detailed prayer. Meanwhile it proves best to bind up the demonic powers that will have gained access through the person's vulnerability. The best time to order the demons out in Jesus' name will be after the stress begins to go.

Significantly, the drug <u>zopiclone</u> seems to dissolve the censor and re-awaken the soul from the inhibition produced by shock and trauma. It seems to re-establish cerebral connections so that the person can function as though the shock and trauma had not occurred. It has even awakened some people from what had seemed to be a permanently vegetative state. However, zopiclone can also be alarmingly disinhibiting and addictive. The better medicine by far is to have regular sessions that include binding associated demons and then touching on the shocking events, with progressive prayer for God's healing in the name of Jesus, in the company of other people who will not themselves be too traumatized by experiences that have to be related.

Memory loss

Amnesia (loss of memory) may be due to head injury, as above, but it may also be due to other medical conditions that damage brain physiology. There is loss of recent and remote memory and reduced ability for new learning. Immediate recall will be preserved, however, and perception and other cognitive functions usually remain intact. But there will be disorientation, particularly in respect of time, and there may be a remarkable facility for confabulation - of various degrees of sophistication - that tries to cover up the vulnerability of being so very lost and forgetful.

Tiny haemorrhages, congestion and swollen cells in nuclei of the limbic system, centrally, close to the brain stem, may be associated with this inability to remember. If left untreated too long, this acute picture may progress to atrophy of these affected parts of the brain.

Such lesions are most notably caused through serious deficiency of B vitamins. Thiamine seems especially necessary for the physiology in the brain nuclei. Lack of sufficiently oxygenated blood may cause similar brain lesions.

The lack of B vitamins may be dietary. A diet including meat and vegetables will contain sufficient vitamins, but famine, or changes in the gut that may be due to cancer of the stomach or persistent vomiting or chronic alcoholism, may cause dangerous deficiency. The latter is the most common cause. The loss of memory can be cured by the injection of B vitamins. Sometimes it is necessary to ask God what food should be eaten!

Transient attacks of loss of memory may also be due to disease of the arteries that supply the brain stem. More permanent memory loss may result from subarachnoid haemorrhage, herpes simplex viral encephalitis, and carbon monoxide or carbon dioxide poisoning and these conditions require emergency medical attention.

All these very physical conditions affect the limbic system in the brain. The effect of damage is to cut off the cognitive functions from the emotions.[86] You could say that the person just ceases to remember and there are clear physical reasons. It just may be possible in the early stage for a little healing to come if someone will afford the time to help the individual make godly sense of reconnecting with the past.

Dementia

Dementia involves not only a loss of memory, but also loss of orientation, comprehension, learning capacity, thinking, calculation, judgement, and language. There is no marked reduction in the actual level of consciousness, however. The condition is usually chronic, with slowly progressive physical changes in the tissues of the brain due to disease. There may also be some degree of apathy, and loss of emotional control and social conscience. An element of delirium may eventually develop.

Dementia may sometimes seem to be a consequence of having lived with subtle personal pressures and stresses. Sometimes the person may have used will power and rules to keep going, and will seem to have neglected the inner truths of their soul. Perhaps they will have lived with the habit of controlling their fear and guilt and other emotions, rather than finding God's healing for them. Then if the need for such defences stops, perhaps due to retirement, bereavement, loneliness, exhaustion, loss of interests, or other changes of circumstance, or sometimes due to an acute illness, the physical changes of dementia begin in the brain. At first they may be quite markedly reversible. So the individual should come before the Lord and take full account of what has been going on in his or her life, and receive the Lord's healing as soon as possible.

If dementia progresses it becomes more and more difficult for relevant issues to be addressed. But a certain degree of peace can

---

[86] The limbic system in the brain controls the emotional response to perception.

come from nursing in familiar surroundings and by avoiding the stress and challenge of problems too difficult to cope with, making it as easy as possible to be orientated, to tell the time and date, and to potter about with familiar interests.

The most commonly known dementia is <u>Alzheimer's disease</u>, which may sometimes start to develop in later middle age. Characteristically the person slowly becomes unusually forgetful, increasingly unable to find the right word, and liable to make mistakes doing things. Life is shortened, and after death, if there is an autopsy, it may be seen that there is atrophy and degeneration of the substance of the brain, and damage at the sites of many neurological connections (tangles of nerve fibrils and amyloid plaques).

<u>Pick's disease</u> is another sort of dementia, similar to Alzheimer's and also starting in later middle age, and particularly affecting speech, with notably eccentric, rebellious and antisocial behaviour, which was previously held in check. The routines of everyday life may not be much affected till later. At autopsy it is found that the frontal and temporal lobes of the brain are particularly affected by atrophic changes.

<u>Vascular dementia</u> may be produced by interference to the blood supply to small parts of the brain, either due to small particles of blood clot or other emboli carried with the blood, or due to bleeding from small blood vessels. The effect is to produce a series of small strokes in which small parts of the brain die. This sort of dementia may sometimes be associated with Parkinson's disease. One is struck down slowly. It may perhaps be found that frustration, disappointment, anger or bitterness have played a part, in which case it is never too late to confess one's sin, receive God's forgiveness and seek his healing.

<u>Huntington's disease</u> is an inherited dementia that manifests in the thirties or forties - after children have been born to parents with the condition. There are pockets of it in occasional families across the world. And although this disease is uncommon, there is a fifty percent chance of inheriting it if one of your parents has

it. But there also seem to be cases with no known family history, presumably due to a mutation of the responsible gene. The family history of the disease may sometimes be hidden because of shame. Involuntary jerky movements (chorea), due to disease damage to distinct nerve tracts in the brain, are associated with deterioration of memory and comprehension. There is often an air of hopelessness and depression, and sufferers are quite often irritable and sometimes violent. I believe the disease must be due to a powerful inherited curse and I know that curses can be broken in the name of Jesus (Galatians 3:13). Furthermore, there has been a suggestion that the curse may work through a small fault in brain physiology, perhaps involving an enzyme, which could perhaps lead medical technology to provide a corrective.

Creutzfeldt-Jakob disease is a progressive dementia that can lead to death within a year or two, caused by an infectious agent transmissible from infected spinal cords of animals.

Undiagnosed syphilis may, after many years, cause atrophy in the brain causing memory defects, reckless behaviour and general loss of competence; but it is unusual to come across this disease nowadays because penicillin kills the spirochaete responsible for this venereal infection.

HIV and trypanosomiasis are other infections that can cause dementia. Brain and central nervous tissue is also destroyed in patches by multiple sclerosis and this may result in irritability and apathy and other personality changes, but there are usually other signs of this disease as well, such as weakness and incoordination.

Dementia is also found when the body does not produce sufficient thyroid hormone, which is essential for metabolism (hypothyroidism). It may also result from deficiency of B vitamins in the diet. These conditions may both actually be seen as physical reactions to chronic fear, stress, worry, anxiety, and other sin, which may be sometimes inherited, and which may be reversed by healing in the name of Jesus.

General consideration of brain function

The brain is the nerve centre for the living individual person in this world and physical damage to brain tissue alters checks and balances. The controls on how personality is expressed are changed, usually by inhibition of certain behaviour and disinhibition of other behaviour. Thus brain damage and brain disease confound the responses of soul and body to spiritual influences and relationships. The usual wide range of personal freedom and accountability is impaired and limited. Regulation and control of thought, emotion and behaviour become inflexibly changed, and the spirit of the person may seem effectively imprisoned or crushed by physical disease. Nevertheless, if that person makes peace with God and accepts the relative limitations produced by disease damage, the godly personality will still shine through.

Cautions about secular services

Health service professionals see much more of these conditions than other people, and the political audit and scrutiny to which health care services are subjected are commonly obstructive in many subtle ways to a Christian approach in the power of Holy Spirit. Christian professionals in such places are mostly reduced to trying to influence the politics by their ethical arguments.

The complexity of these physical causes of mental illness need not be used as an excuse to consider all mental illness as primarily physical, however, or to treat all mental illness with technological medicine and pharmacology. Discernment of the cause of sickness grows with experience in those who love their neighbours as themselves and allow themselves to develop godly empathy. And all sorts of miracles of healing occur in the kingdom of God. So it is necessary for disciples of Jesus to be discerning and careful about what they believe about prognosis, about how they use health services, about the hope they have, and about keeping prayer private.

10

PRACTICALITIES

Personal conditions for healing

As a baby first looks at the mother just after birth, and then begins to thrive, so you must accept the victory Jesus won on the cross. This is the gateway into the kingdom of God (see Mark 10:15, Isaiah 66:13 and 49:15 and John 10:7).

The first thing to do is to seek the merciful face of Almighty God, to whom all things are possible, by confessing your inability to find the answers yourself, and by accepting that he sent his only begotten Son Jesus into this world to be our redeemer and saviour, paying the price for your redemption with his shed blood, and overcoming all the powers of death and destruction on the cross on which he was crucified for you, rising from the dead the third day and then being seen by his disciples and sometimes eating with them for forty days.

There is no need to be afraid of repentance, nor of changes and deliverances thereafter. God will send his Holy Spirit to work out the details in your life. Let the King take up residence in you. Allow him to change your heart and mind as time goes by. Engage in the process of always living in his Spirit by his word so that you may be brought into his rest. Your healing comes by grace through faithfulness to the one who is eternally faithful. This is how he sanctifies you and makes you holy so that you can take your place in his eternal kingdom. Do not allow academic or political ideas to distract you from the truths of his word. Refer everything to him (Mark 12:13-17). Drink from him, and out of you will flow rivers of living water (John 7:37-39).

It says in James that if anyone is in trouble they should pray, and if anyone is sick the elders of the church should pray over the person and anoint the person with oil in the name of Jesus. And it says we should confess our sins to one another and pray for each other so that we may be healed (James 5:13-16). God knows everything that is in our hearts, and he knows the truth of all our experience, and our sins, and our wounds, and our wrong relationships, and our demons. All can be sorted out before God, with each other's help, so that we may be reconciled to him through the cross of his only begotten son, and receive his healing.

Difficulties of secularism

We live in a much more sophisticated society than James did. They had no psychiatrists in those days. They made do with sages and prophets and priests, who may well have done a better job. You only need psychiatrists when society ceases to heed the wisdom of God. Sadly, however, many modern churches respect academics and politicians and professional specialists much more than prophets. And politicians are presuming to take the authority to bind and loose in more aspects of an individual's life than ever before.

Too much reliance on the way the world works reduces faith in how God works. It is time for churches to change. It is time for those who claim to be Christian to be radically hospitable to people seeking the way of Jesus, which is different from the way of the world. It is time for them to live in the reality of Jesus, who is the light of the world that shines in the darkness so that everything hidden will be made known. The fashions and forms and ways of thinking of this world are passing away (1 Corinthians 7:31). Faith needs building his way.

Those who turn to Jesus for healing, and who are seeking greater spiritual maturity with brothers and sisters who truly belong in the kingdom of God, should be astute about their use of this world's health services. As with a broken bone, a splint can be provided by the health services, as it were, but the actual healing comes from Almighty God.

Spiritual issues are not the concern of secular health services. To some extent, perhaps, they used to be in days gone by, in societies that were generally Christian, and where a diversity of faiths was not so commonly found. But now any consideration of personal existential issues (as opposed to physical issues) is often obliged to adjust to the demands of the secular state by accepting humanistic standards. Today we have polyclinics providing efficient technological services for curing symptoms. And although governments may acknowledge that faith assists social cohesiveness and can affect attitudes to medical ethics, secular administrations do not know how the spiritual nature of a faith may actually influence healing.

Christian Hospitality

The Holy Bible makes it clear that righteousness, through which the God of Abraham, Isaac and Jacob is revealed, brings healing, and that this righteousness comes by the grace of God through believing in the person of the Lord Jesus Christ. Therefore it is time for individual Christian churches to bring together a core of people with sufficient maturity for attending to others for healing.

Hospitality is important. This does not mean nice tea parties. It mean loving one's neighbour as one's self, with empathy and generosity, allowing them space to be responsible for their own lives, and to get to a place where they carry their own load (Galatians 6:4), by gently enabling them to hear the word of God for themselves for guidance.

To know who one's neighbour is requires discernment. In Luke 10:36 and 37 Jesus teaches that the neighbour is the one who shows mercy. In other contexts Jesus said, "...whoever is not against you is for you" (Luke 9:50) and another time he said, "He who is not with me is against me and he who does not gather with me scatters" (Luke 11:23). Therefore those without mercy and who are against Jesus may not be included in the hospitality. Nevertheless, according to Matthew 22:10 and Luke 14:23-24

213

some unlikely people will be coming into the kingdom in these last days.

It will be necessary to have safe houses. Each church may need several. People will be coming in from the cold, as it were, and will need mercy and warmth to discover the relative safety of other people living with Jesus. Hopefully they will be able to live through what they must and tell their experience, so that God may bring his forgiveness and release and healing into their lives. Repentance can be re-living the pain in the light of truth – re-pain-tance – in the healing presence of God.

Some people who may have hitherto justified themselves with the help of psychiatric diagnosis, and believed their ungracious behaviour to be a symptom of illness that cannot be helped, may perhaps be given the opportunity to take responsibility for themselves and find real freedom.

However, if a person's behaviour is persistently intolerable, perhaps because of violence, excessive noise, addiction, or deception, they will soon be expected to leave because they will have demonstrated their lack of mercy. They will need secular services. If generosity extends to allowing others to be persistently oppressive it can make other people sick, and be counterproductive.

Such houses do not need staff; but they do need a diversity of about twelve real Christians willing to persevere at living together communally and convivially as a household. And not all of them should be needy. Regularly meeting all together at least twice a week, perhaps over meals, will be essential for opening up and understanding what may be going on. Such meetings are best held in the presence of an elder wise enough to be an acceptable referee and teacher, like Jesus. A person like that makes it safe for things to be said that may not otherwise be said.

Some members of each household would work, some would not; some would be suffering, some broken; and some would have found their healing and be able, in consequence, to offer godly wisdom to others.

When there are difficulties it can be hard to get at the root of what is wrong. But for sure, God knows what it is. In order for you to change and become more holy and whole he may want you to allow it to come into the light. The process can be tortuous, and sometimes painful. But the Holy Spirit will reveal it more easily if there is an hospitable ambience, amongst thoughtful Christians, that is conducive to light being shed on hidden facts of experience that may be painful, embarrassing, confusing or distressing. The Holy Spirit requires people who have relinquished legalism and their own ungodly prejudices. He wants them to be generously hospitable in sincerity and truth for hurting people. He will equip them to withstand the inevitable distresses and tensions in the name of Jesus.

Such places and spaces can provide valuable experience for younger Christians. Living in such a place can be a quick way to turn everyday experience into Biblical understanding and spiritual insight. Then they can tell others, so that church teaching is real and relates to what is going on in the immediate present. What is going on in the wider world can be included, too, of course. This is like the Jewish tradition of Agadah, which is authoritative, spontaneously spoken interpretation of Scripture relevant to the needs and circumstances of the moment.

Some may turn it all into song. And others may use it to inspire things they do or make. Others may use their experience for Christian witness in business. Others may become gifted to evangelise. And people who may have seemed to have nothing to offer for any of the purposes of this world may discover that they have a significant place in God's plans. The whole purpose of such places is to reveal the person of Jesus. And it will attract the people God is inviting into his family. All this builds mature faith.

There is too much of the world in the church these days. And some of the gifts God bestows on people are not appreciated because they are not fashionable. They may even be embarrassing. They may even be diagnosable! However it does not seem to me to be God's plan that everyone in a church should be useful or interesting or even good in this world's terms. In fact I am sure that God wants room amongst his people for sinners to sort themselves out (Psalm 22:24). When diverse characters come together into the name of Jesus, the result does not have to be nice according to worldly standards. There may be many discussions and arguments. But if the Father is worshipped in spirit and truth as a body, unity in Jesus will be manifested. It will be as if the different instruments of an unconventional orchestra are playing a symphony to him together.[87] Even if the world does not like the tune, God will be delighted.

It is our duty to God our Father to allow each person their place (Acts 17:26). Genuine Christian fellowship cannot conform to what is commonly socially admired or even to what is academically comprehended (Romans 12:2, 1 Corinthians 1:27-28) and it is only right in God's sight to include people difficult to understand who may even be sometimes quite disturbing (Isaiah 53:2-3, John 1:5, 1 John 1:8).

God values and knows and loves each one of us equally, so it would be presumptuous to exclude anyone because they have been classified with a certain label by the secular authorities of this world and perhaps judged to be in need of a certain plan of treatment. There is no law (yet) in most countries to dictate that we must consult a state regulated medical practitioner if we feel depressed, although if we should need some length of time off work we shall need a medical certificate unless we have private means. It may not be necessary to have a medical certificate, however, if a suffering person is included in a household where some of the business of the household brings in sufficient money to provide for everyone who belongs there, and where Christian wisdom and kindness may obviate any need for professional nursing, occupational therapy or social work.

---

[87] This is an illustration of Derek Prince's, based on Matthew 18:19-20.

Doctors are in business

We often go to the doctor because we are worried and do not know what to do. Because we want relief, we all too readily believe the doctor knows best. What we usually want is for someone to take the pain and worry away. And when we feel really bad we will pay without much thought, if we can, for whatever quick fixes promise to make us feel good again. So doctors are in business!

However, it is always worthwhile first to tell God what we suffer and to ask him to reveal what we need to know and what we should do. Then it is usually worthwhile to pray with others in the church. After all, it is unlikely that the doctor will give us any of the spiritual guidance we need. Usually he will only do tests to determine whether or not anything serious is wrong and then prescribe symptom-relieving treatment. Of course, it may be as well to be sure about whether or not technological medical intervention is reckoned necessary and, if so, why. That is reassuring.

We do not always have to do something by way of treatment simply because other people are made anxious by an individual's condition or behaviour. Christians have often been tempted into doing something when they have been uncertain about what was going on. It would have been more sincere and honest to have told God that they did not know what to do, and then to have waited on God (see 1 Samuel 14 and 15, 2 Samuel 24:14, Psalm 40:1, Micah 7:7, etc.).

So often we have lost our way because we have not heard him. This calls for repentance. Even if much of the wisdom of our great-grandmothers about how to nurse folk through sickness may seem to have been lost, the basic principles of seeking a place of comfort and safety, loving one's neighbour as oneself (Luke 10:25-37) and getting rid of whatever gets in the way of healing (whether the hindrance be physical or spiritual) hold good.[88] Whether or not it is necessary actually to do something else requires godly discernment and wisdom. Only in emergency is it imperative to do something about another person.

To have treatment foisted upon you, and to be treated objectively by others, can easily feel like manipulation. This may be rather objectionable unless all the reasons are understood and accepted. People in mental distress are particularly sensitive about whether or not their will is being dominated and overridden. Of course, it may be obvious to everyone that their will is not free, and seems to be driven by weird forces. But they should be held responsible for themselves nevertheless. Anything else is condescending, and effectively oppresses the person into abandoning hope for change and resignation from responsibility. Their own judgement and decision should therefore be patiently and painstakingly sought before anything is done. Unless a person is willing, madness can be exacerbated by natural resistance to forcibly having to submit to perceived oppression.

Imposition of treatment is obviously necessary sometimes, however. Unnecessary trauma may be avoided by careful empathetic person to person contact. Regrettably, even this is not always possible. Force does sometimes have to be used for the safety of all concerned.

Medical professionals will take histories and do tests and make deductions about anyone who comes under their management, whether voluntarily of not. They allocate diagnostic categories to individuals and offer logical advice based on their scientific conclusions. Usually, in state-run medical facilities, their advice is calculated to be devoid of any sort of spiritual bias other than that of secular, scientific humanism.

There are times, therefore, particularly in the field of mental illness, when the wisdom which God graciously gives to his

---

[88] Debridement is discussed at greater length in my book *Healing for the Wounded Life*.

people might lead them to take note of secular professional opinion but carefully override it. Admittedly, there are also times when medical technology is very useful.

Meeting

As soon as we start classifying the condition instead of addressing the person we are in danger of becoming objective and abstract, and missing the opportunity for the person to be touched with healing. If we focus on only one abstract facet of a person, moreover, we may fail to meet the actual person.

The key to righteous, effective and godly discernment is real meeting, person to person without prejudice, in the light of the Lord (1 John 1:7). Abstract thinking in categories and formulations, which may be psychological or medical or political, can be seductive, by seeming to give ready answers, but this can miss the point by missing the full story, and it can distort the purposes of God.[89]

Listening to God and trusting in words of knowledge without engaging much with the actual person, as has been very fashionable amongst many Christians, may also actually exclude real meeting.[90] The Holy Spirit requires his words to be personally relevant and given in sincerity and truth, loving one's neighbour as oneself, so that they may touch the individual heart, soul and living body, and have personal meaning and personal consequences (Psalm 73:23-26, Psalm 119:76-77). And he requires those who receive his words to be discerning (Luke 8:18, 9:35).

---

[89] Abstract thinking is discussed at length in my book *Engaging with Reality*.

[90] This is a form of the mistake made by the Nicolaitans, namely spiritualising everything and failing sincerely and truly to recognise a person as physically embodied. It effectively dismisses the living physical body as neither good nor spiritual, and judges it mechanical, inconsequential or even bad. People seeking healing may fail to know themselves accepted, and fail to receive the true touch of God, if they sense they are not sincerely met physical person to physical person with a genuine "Hello!"

219

Once fear and apprehension are driven away by love and truth, person-to-person meeting may yield a sense of what may be hidden away in the dark in someone's life. Sharing personal experience with other people who can be trusted opens the heart and mind to receive God's healing. Sharing in groups under godly authority with others who have known similar experiences includes more people in the healing process and may make it more efficient.

Impediments to meeting

If what is shared should be unjustly condemned, or diagnosed, however, it may cease to be possible to share openly. Legalistic condemnation inhibits freedom of speech, because it causes fear and rejection to close the heart, which may then easily become hardened. Whilst it may be right with God to challenge someone's perception, it will be wrong to deny it. Jesus tells us not to condemn out of hand (Matthew 7:1-2). A person is entitled to see things their way, and we are obligated to bring all aspects into the light in God's presence and to seek his peace (1 Corinthians 1:10).

In the fellowship of Christian believers, the effect of one person upon another may be brought into the light and reconciled to God equitably, and this is an essential part of healing (1 John 1:7). No one can deny that each individual has an effect on others (1 Corinthians 12:26). If people are honest with each other it always helps greatly. One day all our behaviour will have to be accounted for before the throne of God, so it seems best to clear things up as soon as possible.

Drugs, both prescribed and illegal, are a subtle and serious hindrance to accountability and to communal fellowship. People will make all sorts of excuses that avoid the truth of why they take them, however, and their self-justifications will commonly be backed up by the medical profession. Although it may be possible to proceed with healing work with an individual whilst that person continues to take prescribed medication, and to ask

220

God to heal the body and to overcome the person's need for drugs, continuing medication will eventually block further work. In fact, to some extent a Christian community will always be less than ideal if members take drugs of any sort.

Drug addiction is often hidden. Secret activity that takes priority over everything else is constantly and obsessively directed to maintaining the supply. The drugs distort perception and reasoning. Although the person may seem to be free they are not. If they are not challenged, and can get away with it, people who persist in taking drugs will force other people to be tacitly complicit in maintaining their self-justification and camouflage. Sooner or later their demons will force them to extend their low life in complex ways that are hidden from the fellowship. Whilst such people may be afforded a modicum of hospitality, they need to be kept on the edge of the society to avoid serious disruption. Their issues will need deliverance if ever they become truly willing.

Seriously demonized people, too, can be exceedingly disruptive. Satan uses them to destroy churches. And this includes those we naturally feel sorry for as well as those who are criminal. It includes those with whom it is impossible to have an open conversation, and those who have been in psychiatric or other hospital care for years and just want hand-outs. They can be met with love but with circumspection. Jesus did not speak with demons other than to tell them to be silent or command them out, and people who know the Lord have the authority to behave the same way. Far from being unkind, this may actually help people to recognise the Lord Jesus. Those who will come to him for healing are those who will be set free to join the fellowship.

So it may be necessary to be very firm and occasionally to expel people (1 Corinthians 5). It is human nature to test the boundaries to see how far it is possible to go. But people feel safer if they know the limits are authentic and hold firm. Sanctions may be imposed on behaviour that is intolerable or not adequately accounted for, and therefore not reconciled to God (1

Corinthians 5). Neither social pressures nor punishments nor sanctions, however, can force a person to change; but those who prove to be unwilling or unable to be sufficiently accountable to maintain their credibility within the fellowship before God may need to leave for the sake of the honour of God's name. The demands made on all the people involved can sometimes be severe.

Walking in the light

If there is to be healing through bringing out into the light what has been hidden in the dark, it is necessary for truth to be spoken in godly love. And it is also necessary for the people involved in leadership to be mature enough not to be seriously wounded by any material that may become exposed, nor by anything that may happen. It is important for them to be sufficiently healed themselves automatically to react in righteous ways no matter what is thrown at them. And it will be necessary for them to know they can pray to God in the highest heaven and be heard, and that they can take authority in the name of Jesus over the activity of unclean spiritual powers to bind them from hindering what the Lord is doing.

During the process of healing it is necessary to a large extent for personal experience to be told in speech. The language does not have to be perfect. The speech that counts is that which connects the heart and mind of the person in significant detail with others who hear, and especially with God, so that how it was, and how it is, will be told. It may be necessary to have the help of others to achieve this. If the Lord is present, he will not only be the judge, in truth, of what is expressed, but he will also be the healer. Coming together into the name of Jesus to share like this brings his presence into the meeting (Matthew 18:20) and his authority will be present for those who lead, and then whatever is not right before the cross of Christ can be put right (John 5:22) because it is through him that we find healing (2 Corinthians 3:16 – 4:2 and 10:5).

Personal, sincere, truthful meeting, however, is not always easy for people who have been diagnosed with mental illness, because they will often have been made to feel abnormal, and therefore they will secretly feel unworthy and become frightened of implicit accusations and of further rejection. Consequently they may dissemble and avoid sincerity. They may even be so used to insincerity that they view everything with suspicion, and consequently fail to take hold of godly truth. Nevertheless, everyone's experience (whether diagnosable or not) can always be interpreted biblically in the Spirit and with godly love, and we may not know when God's words are actually received in the heart.

We live in a fallen world in which none of us is perfect. The injunction to love our neighbours as ourselves applies to people who fail to fit our idea of perfection, just as we fail to fit God's. Generosity, hospitality and loving acceptance of each other's mess is kindness, which is a gift of the Holy Spirit (Galatians 5:22). Kindness is recognition that we who meet in Jesus are of the same kind. Kindness generates hope and encouragement. These are essential for healing.

Religious Culture

The culture of churches needs to change from being the culture of a social club, led by moral and ethical rules and the politics of institutional religion, into the culture of an army led by Holy Spirit, engaged in a spiritual war against the fallen world, death and Satan.

Those who belong in the kingdom of God are those who have made the Lord Jesus Christ king in their lives. We are engaged in bringing in and defending the eternal kingdom of the living God.

Although the enemy was defeated by our King Jesus on the cross, the devil is still seducing many people into destruction and a living death. A continuing war is still being fought over individual souls. He is fighting a desperate last ditch stand to convince as many people as possible that his defeat is not real.

223

The battle will not be pretty. His defeat has to be made good by us in these days.

The battle for hearts and minds will not be truly won if all that is done is subtly to impose compliance to some sort of Christian culture, with its social games and politics. What counts is people coming to personal faith in Jesus, taking hold of him, and then proving themselves to be set free from sin, and justified by their faith in him, in every aspect of their lives (James 2:14-26). This will attract others.

People who begin to turn to Jesus are often traumatized, troubled and confused. And in order to make Jesus credible thy need the help of other people who have known Jesus well. Psychiatric clinics are not the place for them. Faith has to be nurtured in every area of experience in order to be proved real, and to allow sound maturity to develop. Jesus is utterly relevant for the healing of the traumas, troubles, sicknesses and confusions of everyone, and for bringing them into freedom.

So a change is needed inside each person who dares to be called Christian, an opening up of how the mind was previously made up, a letting go of inadequate assumptions, and a willingness to be taught new things by the Holy Spirit in order to become equipped for challenging times. In other words, repentance is needed within the church. Restoration is needed – something much more profound than previous reformations.

The habit of caring for the sick out of what are nowadays called pity and sympathy has to go. The devil hijacked the true meaning of these concepts of pity and sympathy long ago, just as he hijacked the concept of charity. He turned them into attitudes that can be adopted without really allowing yourself to know in your spirit what the other person is going through, in other words without real empathy. So you give money to appease your guilt because you do not really want to know the hell of the other person's suffering. Indeed the suffering in this world is so very much too much for any of us to cope with that it may seem that there is little else we can do but give money to appease the demands of the poor who have no knowledge of God.

Without knowing Jesus we cannot begin to face allowing ourselves to have real true godly disinterested compassion for human wretchedness. But when we know Jesus we know the man who really took up our infirmities and carried our sorrows and overcame them all. By his wounds we are healed (Isaiah 53). Therefore we can take our place with others in doing what he is doing, and we can intercede. Although this may involve suffering ourselves, our God will see us through (Philippians 3:10).

The only attitude that proves truly credible is real Christian empathy, which is in fact loving your neighbour as yourself with devotion to God. When this is apparent the suffering person knows that you know - as when Jesus touched and healed the leper (Mark 1:41). With such compassion, kindness is tempered with wisdom, and with authority and self-control. This is not simple philanthropy, for the Bible teaches that Jesus only did what his father was doing (John 5:19) and knew what was in a person (John 2:25) and acted accordingly, and the Holy Spirit will likewise reveal to us what we need to know, where we should be, and what we should say and do. So when Jesus spoke with the woman at the well (John 4:29) his speech was "full of grace, seasoned with salt" (Colossians 4:6). You can only show this sort of compassion when you, too, have suffered (Hebrews 2:10-13).

So it is necessary for people in churches to sort themselves out through seeking their own salvation, with repentance and deliverance, led by the Holy Spirit, allowing the Lord to heal them. They will hopefully have travelled a good long way in this process before being available to many others. Mind you, being with others as they find their healing can challenge you to find yours. What really counts is a humble, teachable attitude, open to new moves of the Spirit, and a personal willingness to change inwardly oneself. Without maturity, however, serious mistakes could be made.

Churches that do not gear in to this sort of work may be in very serious danger of losing the oil for their lamps (Matthew

25:1-13). It is easier to ignore the need to be replenished with Holy Spirit if unpleasant aspects of reality are avoided. Personal involvement with each other's troubles, and bearing each other's burdens so that each may carry their own load (Galatians 6:2-5), brings home the relevance of the word of God to each individual involved and, perhaps unexpectedly, this becomes a source of encouragement and joy. Conversely, dealing with everyday issues theoretically and impersonally through programmes strictly according to policy protocols does not build the personal holiness necessary for the bride to meet the bridegroom. The work needs to touch and affect the heart in immediate context, and be worked out in ordinary everyday living. If church culture is alive in the Lord, everyone can be doing serious business with God concerning their own souls at any time. Dealing with one's own personal issues through seeking the face of God, forgiveness and healing, and at the same time helping others to find their healing, and thus building informal churches of people who know their redeemer for real, is what will gather those who are going to the wedding banquet (Isaiah 25, Matthew 22, Luke 14).

Apparent crises

What comes up for healing can sometimes be suddenly turbulent. The medical profession has always known that healing comes either through lysis or through crisis. It is similar both with physical healing and with spiritual healing. Lysis is a loosening and gradual attenuation and dissolving of the trouble. If lysis is proceeding well, crisis does not always occur. But sometimes a freak out or crisis seems inevitable, even perhaps necessary.

This sort of thing was seen more frequently in the days before the symptoms of illness were so effectively suppressed with drugs, most notably in the days before antibiotics. A serious infection like pneumonia would either slowly subside or, alternatively, would reach an acute crisis in which the infection would be overcome with gross perspiration and delirium, leaving the patient either exhausted (but healing) or dead.

Although crises can be prevented with drugs these days, in the field of mental distress and psychiatry this may not always be in a person's best interests, because drugs may prevent the necessary loosening up of the mind's prejudices and strongholds, and hinder the change of mind which true healing brings. Spiritual healing takes place through revelation. It is not corrective experience that heals and changes people, but rather revelation. But there is always resistance to revelation until it appears - it is always darkest just before the dawn. And it appears when God deems the person ready to receive it. The resistance may be worn away gradually as revelation comes to the person piecemeal – and this is lysis. Or occasionally there may be a sudden crisis if resistance to everything connected with the revelation has been intense but is finally being overcome, as happened with Paul (Acts 9). Something similar also seems to have happened to Ezekiel, who was utterly overwhelmed for a whole week after seeing visions of God (Ezekiel 3:15).

Of course, counterfeit revelations may be given to some people if demonic spirits have access to the person. It is very definitely only the revelation given by Holy Spirit that is truly healing. Careful discernment is necessary. Any Christian going through a crisis therefore needs the protection and the prayers of others.

So contrary to the opinions of this world, there seems to be a place for crises. Of necessity vulnerable individuals going through a crisis should be carefully protected in the Lord. And it can be a mistake to look to secular authorities for help, unless the person going through the crisis refuses the Lord Jesus or unless the Lord is discerned not to be in it. The person going through the crisis should be in a safe place where secular authorities are unlikely to interfere, and the person should be protected from injuring his or her person, or anyone else, by the careful attention of others. Musical instruments should be banned because (from experience!) music can be either immediately and intensely seductive or profoundly disturbing and can lead the person astray. Television, media and computers should be banned, too, for similar reasons. And going outside will be a very bad idea because the outside world cannot be trusted in these situations. Otherwise that person will need the freedom to eat, sleep, do this and do that, for as long as the Spirit takes in his dealings with that person. The loving care of about twelve mature Christians working in shifts will probably be found to be the best way.

The person may be very stressed, torn apart, confused, even deluded, or hallucinating and caught in the opposing forces of their lives so that they cease, by and large, to relate to the world outside of themselves for a while. That outside world only seems to threaten to tear them apart more. They may become so stressed and vulnerable as to be almost unable to distinguish between without and within. They may hear voices, or see visions. The effects of influences upon them may seem exaggerated or weird. There may be catharsis, and demons may manifest and be expelled. There may be a very major rearrangement of the mind as the Lord's healing takes place. If the process is unencumbered, however, and those around them remain truthful, prayerfully and authoritatively waiting on the Lord, the crisis will not usually last more than two weeks or so, often less. Paul's lasted three days. And afterwards they will probably be quite all right.

Many notable Christians have been through spiritual crises. Meister Eckhart, John of the Cross, Bruder Klaus, Catherine of Genoa, Teresa of Avila, Richard Rolle, Henry Suso, Hugo St. Victor, George Fox, and some of the early Methodists, and many others, have heard the word of God preached and have come under the power of the Holy Spirit and become "distressed for full salvation". Their crises changed their lives, and in consequence enabled many other lives to be changed, too, through the revelation of Jesus. Such people may not have been as purely empowered by the Holy Spirit as the prophets and saints of the Bible but they had enormous influence. It is interesting and relevant to speculate how psychiatrists may have treated them if it had been as fashionable in their day as it is today to diagnose and sedate. [91]

Care must be exercised, however. There are many people these days who are actively seeking spiritual empowerment through contrived and apparently sanitised crises of one sort or another. In the oppressive world of human rights and political control of religion there seems to be a reactive, rebellious hunger for spiritual power from any and every source. Folk go to special places to allow themselves to become vulnerable, expecting power to be imparted through certain spiritually anointed people. What determines whether or not these people fall into some illness or accident or folly is both the extent of the vulnerability of their minds and the true nature of the spiritual influence they receive. This sort of thing even happens in the name of "Jesus". Who the Jesus truly is, however, is often debatable. It behoves Christians, therefore, to be most carefully discerning. Everywhere there is a great deal of brilliantly subtle deception, even in churches.

What is often forgotten is that it is God who decides when and where and in whom his Spirit shall move (John 3:8). To pre-empt him is therefore presumptuous.

People who feel weak may seek to gain spiritual power without counting the cost (Luke 14:28) and without sufficient discernment (Proverbs 11:14; 15:22; 24:6). What they usually lack is faith. Power would be given if they were patient in waiting on God (Psalm 116). Paul said, "...when I am weak, then I am strong" (2 Corinthians 12:10). He had experience of how the Lord brings us through when all seems lost. In specific situations faith may be lacking because various types of sorcery, theories, alternative belief systems, drugs, media, technological conveniences, and so on, successfully obscure truth. There is even a fashion for believing that Christians need not suffer. This is

---

[91] The philosopher Karl Jaspers(1883-1969) said Ezekiel was schizophrenic! Note Hosea 9:7.

suggested in the NIV translation of the prayer of Jabez in 1 Chronicles 4:9-10. But this interpretation is contradicted by Paul's comment to Timothy (recorded in 2 Timothy 3:12) that, "In fact everyone who wants to live a godly life in Christ Jesus will be persecuted."

The meaning of illness

The trouble with avoiding suffering by suppressing all the symptoms, and trying to continue as normal with the help of pills, injections, surgery and all the modern medical technology, but without consulting God, is that in consequence we may lose our way without knowing it. This does not mean that we should not use technological medicine, just that we should be astute about how we use it, because there is always more to our condition than medicine can resolve.

Although I accept this may not be the full story (as witness the story of Job, and also those caught in epidemics), I assume as a rule of thumb that any illness I may develop could be a result of the way I have lived and of what has been going on in my life, and in the lives of my ancestors. Therefore if I become ill I shall seek God's help to examine myself for specific sin, for wounds that need healing, for relationships that may be wrong in some way in God's sight, and for demons that need expelling. I shall wait on God for his mercy and provision concerning such matters and see what he will reveal and bring into my mind through my suffering. Whether I discover any such antecedents or not, I shall consult appropriate church elders and ask them to pray for me and to anoint me with oil (as recommended in James 5:14).

God has mercy on those on whom he will have mercy (Exodus 33:19). This helps us understand something of the meaning of John 9:3 where the significant point Jesus makes is not that the blind man or his ancestors have sinned (for we are all sinners), but that God is having mercy on him by opening his eyes in healing so that God's glory may be revealed. The healing we should seek is not necessarily that all our apparent defects should

230

be eradicated but rather that our eyes and ears should be opened and we should know him in our hearts. Then we might be surprised at how we are changed.

If I fail to use my illness to take account of my life, I may lose my way. If I dismiss my illness as nothing to do with any of my sin, and a nuisance to be eradicated without using it for repentance, I may be ignoring an opportunity to sort something out about my life that the Lord would then have to bring to my attention another way, which might be worse. Repentance is more than just making confession and asking forgiveness, it is also a process of actively renewing the mind in order to overcome. Then the account eventually given to God (Romans 11:32 - 12:2, 2 Peter 1:3-10) will be to his glory.

Because sin is reactive, it sometimes makes us seriously ill. Full repentance involves going over events from the past that seem to be connected with present events, and being flexible enough to change habits. Faith has to be built by applying the word of God to past and present personal experience, whether or not it is diagnosable by secularists, and whether or not healing is received. Unless the Lord is taken hold of in this way, maturity in the faith is compromised. Sanctification like this is necessary because "…without holiness no one will see the Lord" (Hebrews 12:14).

In these end times so much is being ignored, with the help of drugs and media and other technological conveniences, that whole churches are losing their way and thus failing to shepherd their people safely. You can have a lot of pleasure when you feel good but the "feel-good factor" is not to be trusted, "For wide is the gate and broad is the road that leads to destruction, and many enter through it" (Matthew 7:13). Some people cannot even bear to be alone and quiet, unless they have taken their medication, because they have lost contact with God and neglected his word. Myriad enticements are at hand to convince us, if possible, that Jesus could never be the way to find release from torment.

How can we return to God without admitting we have lost our way? How can we hear his voice if we drown it out with distractions because it is uncomfortable? How can we suffer the discomfort without faith? How can we find our way again without recognising that we have lost it and calling on him to save us (Psalm 107)? How can the fruit of faith be found in our lives (Galatians 5:22) without allowing ourselves to know he suffers with us through the trials he has permitted, and that he heals us to reveal his glory that he may be known?

Both Israel and also the first Christians were family (Isaiah 63:1, Mark 3:34-35), an intimate community of households wherein healing and redemption could be found through returning to God. It is now time to come together into his healing "...for the Lord's renown, for an everlasting sign which will not be destroyed" (Isaiah 55:13).

"Return to me," declares the Lord Almighty, "and I will return to you," says the Lord Almighty (Zechariah 1:3).

BIBLIOGRAPHY

Both secular and Christian books are included in this list, which is for corroboration rather than for clear guidance. Please let the Holy Spirit and the words of the Holy Bible be your guide.

Published biographical accounts of schizophrenia
Barnes, M. & Berke, J. (1971) 'Mary Barnes: Two Accounts of a Journey Through Madness', New York, Ballantine Books.

Bateson, G. (editor) (1974) 'Perceval's Narrative', New York, William Morrow & Co. (This is John Perceval's account of the schizophrenia he suffered between 1830-1832, originally written in two volumes published in 1838 and 1840 in London by Effingham Wilson, and edited in this edition by Gregory Bateson. John Perceval was the fifth son of Spencer Perceval, the Christian Prime Minister of England murdered in 1812.)

Boisen, A.T. (1936) 'The Exploration of the Inner World', U.S.A., Willet, Clark & Company. (Anton Boisen became a Baptist minister.)

Coate, M. (1964) 'Beyond All Reason', London, Constable & Co.

Cockburn, Patrick and Henry (2011) 'Henry's Demons', London, Simon & Schuster (UK) Ltd.

Conran, M. (1999) 'Sorrow, Vulnerability and Madness' in 'Psychosis (Madness)' edited by Paul Williams, London, Institute of Psycho-Analysis.

Greenberg, J., alias Green, H., (1964) 'I Never Promised You a Rose Garden', London, Gollancz.

Kaplan, B. (editor) (1964) 'The Inner World of Mental Illness', New York, Harper & Row.

Laing, R.D. (1960) 'The Divided Self', London, Tavistock Publications (the cases of Peter, Julie, James, and Rose).

Laing, R.D. (1967) 'The Politics of Experience', London, Penguin Books (the case of Jesse Watkins).

233

Oakley, H. (1989) 'Touching and being touched' in Cooper, R., et al., 'Thresholds between Philosophy and Psychoanalysis (Papers from the Philadelphia Association)', London, Free Association Books.

O'Brien, B. (1958) 'Operators and Things', London, Elek Books Ltd.

Stacey, J. (2004) 'Schizophrenia Defeated', Bromsgrove, Crossbridge Books.

Biographical accounts of depression

Facius, J. (1990) 'God Can Do It Without Me', Tonbridge, Sovereign World.

Lewis, G. (2002) 'Sunbathing in the Rain', Great Britain, Flamingo.

Solomon, A. (2002) 'The Noonday Demon', London, Vintage.

Styron, W. (1991) 'Darkness Visible', Great Britain, Jonathan Cape.

A biographical account of obsessional illness

Cooper, R. (1989) 'Dwelling and the 'therapeutic community'', in Cooper, R., et al., 'Thresholds between Philosophy and Psychoanalysis (Papers from the Philadelphia Association)', London, Free Association Books.

Biographical accounts of hysteria

Freud, S. and Breuer, J. (1893-5) 'Studies on Hysteria' in The Standard Edition of 'The Complete Psychological Works of Sigmund Freud', translated under the editorship of James Strachey, Volume 2, London, Hogarth Press, 1955.

A biographical account of personality disorder

Bramhall, C. (2005) 'Am I A Good Girl Yet?' Oxford, Monarch Books.

A biographical account about the healing of addiction

Pullinger, J. (1980) 'Chasing the Dragon', Hodder.

Books about deliverance

Basham, D. (1972) 'Deliver us from Evil', Grand Rapids: Chosen Books. ISBN 0-8007-9069-3.

Hammond, F. & I.M. (1973) 'Pigs in the Parlour', Kirkwood, Missouri, Impact Books, Inc.

Prince, Derek (1998) 'They Shall Expel Demons', Baldock, Derek Prince Ministries. ISBN 1-901144-06-2.

Horrobin, P. (1994 & 1995) 'Healing Through Deliverance', 2 Vols., Lancaster, Sovereign World. ISBNs 1-85240-052-8 & 1-85240-039-0.

Other books about healing

Prince, Derek: 'God's Word Heals', DPM-UK Baldock (2010) ISBN 978-1-901144-48-2.

Wright, H.W. 'A More Excellent Way', Thomaston, Georgia, USA, Pleasant Valley Church, Inc. ISBN 978-0-9678059-2-4 (www.beinhealth.com).

Gordon, Dr John (2007) 'Healing for the Wounded Life', Seaford, Thankful Books/Philadelphia Books. ISBN 978-1-905084-10-4.

Gordon, J.F. (2012) 'Schizophrenia', Philadelphia Books. ISBN 978-0-9570970-2-5.

INDEX

Page numbers in *italics* refer to 'Healing for the Wounded Life' ISBN 978-1-905084-10-4, 253pp, £9.95, published in 2007 by Philadelphia Books (www.philadelphiabooks.co.uk).

Page numbers in **bold type** refer to this book,' Healing the Divided Self,' which is the sequel.

About the Author

John Gordon qualified in medicine from Cambridge University, and subsequently trained in the Wessex School of Psychiatry whilst serving in the Royal Navy at Royal Victoria Hospital, Netley. Later he was a psychiatrist at Warlingham Park Hospital, Surrey. Then he worked privately in London and trained in psychoanalytic psychotherapy under R.D.Laing and H.A.Crawford in the Philadelphia Association. After qualifying he was elected to Membership; but he soon resigned as humanistic philosophy became preponderant. He moved to Devon to work part-time as a psychotherapist leading a therapeutic community in the National Health Service, and part-time as a GP. Later he joined the prison service. After managing a psychiatric unit (known as 'Fraggle Rock' to the locals) in Preston prison, he led one of the therapeutic communities in Grendon prison.

Over many years he has been guided by Holy Spirit to develop a Christian understanding of emotional and mental suffering, pain, confusion and perversity that accords with the Biblical nature of mankind and the relationship with the only wise God who heals described in Judeo-Christian scripture. Although account is taken of scientific insight, this differs from secular psychology and psychiatry. His books are: 'Healing for the Wounded Life', 'Healing the Divided Self', 'Schizophrenia', and 'Engaging with Reality'.

John and Pamela are licensed members of The Order of Jacob's Well. They have been married since 1965 and have a Christian family.